MARRY YES
MARRY NO

MARRY YES MARRY NO
Marriage for the clueless

DR. MARI P. SAUNDERS

LitPrime Solutions
21250 Hawthorne Blvd
Suite 500, Torrance, CA 90503
www.litprime.com
Phone: 1 (209) 788-3500

© 2021 Dr. Mari P. Saunders. All rights reserved.

No part of this book may be reproduced, stored in a retrieval system, or transmitted by any means without the written permission of the author.

Published by LitPrime Solutions   05/21/2021

ISBN: 978-1-954886-57-5(sc)
ISBN: 978-1-954886-58-2(e)

Library of Congress Control Number: 2021912920

Any people depicted in stock imagery provided by iStock are models, and such images are being used for illustrative purposes only.

Certain stock imagery © iStock.

Because of the dynamic nature of the Internet, any web addresses or links contained in this book may have changed since publication and may no longer be valid. The views expressed in this work are solely those of the author and do not necessarily reflect the views of the publisher, and the publisher hereby disclaims any responsibility for them.

CONTENTS

Acknowledgments vii

Preface. ix

Chapter 1   The Case for Pre-marital Counseling 1

Chapter 2   The Other 23 Hours 5

Chapter 3   Know Thyself 13

Chapter 4   Your Emotional Health 23

Chapter 5   The Dance of Males and Females. 35

Chapter 6   The Dynamics of Couple Therapy. 41

Chapter 7   Reshaping Your Female Attitudes. 51

Chapter 8   Reshaping Your Male Attitudes 65

Chapter 9   She Says, He Hears, He Says, She Hears. 71

Chapter 10 It Is The Small Stuff That Counts 77

Chapter 11 The Potential Extension of Marriage – Children 85

Chapter 12 Compatibility Quiz 89

Chapter 13 What's Your E.Q.? 95

Chapter 14 Rules of Thumb for Men Before Considering
            Marriage 115

Chapter 15 Rules of Thumb for Females Before Considering
            Marriage 121

Chapter 16 Off The Cuff (The way I see it) 127

Appendix. 135

ACKNOWLEDGMENTS

I want, need, have to, posthumously thank Dr. Thomas M. Johnson, a gifted psychologist.

Without him, I would not, could not, have journeyed down my own road of self-discovery which turned out to be simultaneously terrifying and illuminating. He saw in me what I barely saw in myself. He was not only my therapist but also my mentor and inspired me to ultimately become his colleague. I cannot imagine what my life would have been like without him.

To Cecily without whose help, intelligence, patience, good nature, tolerance, insight and understanding this work would not have been completed. We've come a long way baby!

PREFACE

Ten good reasons for getting pre-marital counseling (not necessarily in this order):
1. The decision not to be married needs to be reached before you marry—not afterwards. On-the-job training doesn't always work!
2. It's cheaper financially or emotionally and it will probably take less time than seeing a marriage counselor, filing for divorce, or resorting to other drastic measures.
3. You will have something else working for you besides your hormones.
4. You will get to know yourself and your partner in ways you would never have known otherwise.
5. Charity begins at home; so do wars. There's no such thing as a one-sided coin.
6. Any decision you make about getting married will at least be an informed one.
7. Really being in touch with yourself and accepting your own feelings, flaws, and convictions—whether you marry or not—will add years to your life.
8. Nobody likes nasty little surprises, especially those which conflict with your previous perceptions and illusions. It pays to be prepared.
9. You will collect a lot of valuable information, insights, strategies, and possible solutions for future use when things go bump in the night—as they are bound to do.
10. Although there will always be exceptions to the rule, generally a happy, healthy marriage will produce emotionally healthy and well-balanced children.

CHAPTER 1

The Case for Pre-marital Counseling

And they lived happily ever after. Or did they? How many times has that tag line been drummed into our subconscious? How about from toddlerhood—when we were being read to—until we began reading for ourselves. Consider the source. The phrase was generally at the end of a fairy tale—which rarely, if ever, included an epilogue.

Subliminally it creeps under our conscious cover that marriage or the commitment to live with another human being as a mate or partner is the beginning of an ideal existence that is expected to bring great comfort, joy and bliss. It is also supposed to banish the demons of loneliness and to discourage negative societal opinions and attitudes about one's single state while simultaneously attracting the approbation and sly smiles of almost everyone. All the world loves a lover. Our predecessors, teachers and role models leave out the message that in actuality, marriage also is often the beginning of an eye opening experience fraught with emotional cobblestones. Everything contains its own opposite. There is no such thing as a one-sided coin.

IS MARRIAGE THE SOLUTION TO EVERYTHING?
There are so many of us who have been brainwashed to believe that marriage is the solution not only to our loneliness but also to many of our personal problems. We are therefore not inclined to deal with emotional detour signs especially when, or if, our hormones are kicking in. When the unanticipated underside of marriage rears its ugly head,

we quickly become disillusioned, frustrated, resentful, disgusted and often downright hostile about what we discover. One could readily attribute these reactions to the fact that we had no conscious preparation or guidelines that would help us negotiate our way through the river of our own negative feelings.

The term "conscious" is significant here because of the marriage blue prints and designs that were indelibly implanted in our subconscious while we were growing up. There is that tendency to repeat in our marriage what we were exposed or subjected to in the marriage of our parents, caretakers or meaningful others in our lives. There are not many people who will sit down and ponder, investigate or ask themselves or each other how each of them perceived or experienced the marriage of their parents. Nevertheless these feelings, attitudes and experiences play a very large role in how their own marriages will fare.

IRONING OUT THE KINKS AHEAD OF TIME

It's no secret that the divorce rate is up to 55% or 60%. Its escalation has been staring us all in the face for the past 25-30 years with seemingly very little hope of diminishing. "An ounce of prevention" would appear to apply here. One of the ways of possibly lowering this rate is to be willing to do some consequential thinking in terms of avoiding getting initially involved in what could potentially be a disastrous marriage. The toll divorce has been known to take emotionally, financially, as well as physically on its participants can be awesome, especially where there are children involved. The scars, feelings of deprivation, depression, hostility and any number of other negative reactions it causes can, and often do last a life time. Human nature being what it is, people are going to continue to marry (hope springs eternal) for all the wrong reasons. On the upside, there will be those who either get lucky or have the motivation and perseverance to ride out the speed bumps. They are also willing to put a great deal of time and effort into a repair job that enables them to go the distance, however rocky a road that might turn out to be. This may be doing it the hard way but it can and often does work. Getting the jump on hindsight, which is always 20-20, and putting forth this effort before a legal or other binding commitment has been made, definitely raises a couple's chances of either discovering they are not meant for each other or offering them the opportunity of ironing out a lot of kinks in their relationship before marrying. This process alone enables them to set the stage for workable solutions to problems that will undoubtedly emerge after marriage.

DYSFUNCTIONAL TRENDS

If anyone needs motivation for understanding and dealing with one's partner before making an ultimate commitment, one need only take a good, hard look at some current statistics. At least 75% of incarcerated criminals grew up without a father, father figure or had an abusive parent of either sex. In many cases they were in a home where they had experienced the separation or death of a parent leaving only one stressed out parent, usually a mother. More than likely they were products of dysfunctional families, which produce dysfunctional human beings. Without therapy or some other type of intervention, these victims often find it difficult to survive emotionally and often end up creating yet another dysfunctional family.

We may grow too old too soon and too late smart but who's to say we can't manipulate the statistics and stack the odds more in our favor? We can begin by understanding something about the dynamics involved in the dance of males and females and such knowledge can hopefully help us compliment each other rather than influence us to be at odds with each other.

BEING OBJECTIVE

It's easy to be objective about a relationship when you're not in one, and just about impossible to be objective when you are. So, if you are not in a serious relationship right now, as you read this you are probably in better emotional shape to absorb and process the contents of the next few chapters. If you are in a relationship that you are considering turning into a marriage—your ability to profit from any of these ideas will depend upon a lot of factors. The most significant of these is your emotional maturity which includes how realistic you are about yourself, and your perceptions and expectations of others. There are many tests and quizzes (some of which will appear in a later chapter) that will give you some clues and general information about yourself. The case for knowing, understanding and accepting oneself (which also enables one to know and understand one's partner better) cannot be overstated. A large part of premarital counseling is helping the individual involved to become acquainted with all the dimensions of his or her persona on an individual as well as on a couple basis. Getting to know the light and dark side of one's own personality is not always a welcome choice. However, if we can't tolerate the downside of ourselves we will never be able to handle similar truths in our meaningful other. The role that an intimate relationship plays in our physical and emotional well-being is well established. Simultaneously anything we perceive as robbing us of our independence or autonomy (and intimacy often confuses this issue) causes us anxiety and sometimes panic. The need to be autonomous, in control of ourselves and our fate conflicts with our basic need for closeness, security and trust with another human being. The psychic energy used to deal with this dilemma is often depleted to the point of our behaving rather badly in relationships or worse, rendering us incapable of functioning productively in any relationship we happen to fall into or believe we consciously want on any sustained basis. The problems abound when we discover we are already in a committed situation we don't necessarily want to get out of for whatever rewards it offers, but we don't function well or properly in the relationship either.

There's never going to be a definitive course of action or a strategy or formula that will guarantee a healthy, happy marriage. If you were an A+ student in medical school, at the top of your class, once you get in the real world, you will constantly be challenged by medical cases that will put every skill you have to the task of solving or curing the presenting problem. No matter how knowledgeable or skillful you are, you will not always have an answer. The vagaries of human nature are such that there will also be situations for which you are not intellectually or emotionally prepared. However, as in any endeavor, going in armed with self knowledge, information, tolerance, as much of a positive attitude as you can muster and a willingness to work at unanticipated problems will go a long way toward maintaining what can be the best or the worst of human endeavors.

CHAPTER 2

The Other 23 Hours

One of my new patients came into our office without her significant other. As she put it, she only wanted to determine if she and her intended really needed pre-marital counseling. She was informed that pre-marital counseling was for couples and that it was ineffective without the presence, opinions, attitudes and contributions of both parties. She glided by this explanation and went on to describe how compatible she and her mate were especially sexually. She extolled his virtues as a lover and gave a few examples of how they would often slip away from their jobs and meet on their lunch hour to have what she coyly referred to as a "nooner."

I asked her what they did for the other twenty-three hours. At first she seemed somewhat taken aback at the question. However, she rallied quickly replying that they didn't see that much of each other during the week because each of them held important positions on their jobs and led busy lives. She explained that whenever they could get together on a weekend day, they made the effort to put aside their personal projects in order to spend quality time with each other. When asked what they did on the weekends, she acknowledged that they did spend a good deal of the time in bed. Back to square one. I asked the question again "so what do you do for the other twenty three hours?" I then tried to get across to her that the other twenty three hours was a metaphor of what marriage was really all about.

During a brief discussion, I ran down a list of concerns, and decisions that end up being the very essentials of a good marriage. She had not touched upon any of them during our talk. It was at this point, she appeared to be somewhat overwhelmed by it all and asked if my partner would sit in on our next session because she intended to bring in her fiancé.

This does not mean that clients are not seen on an individual basis, especially in those instances where personal and individual conflicts or problems have not been resolved. Potential spouses cannot be expected to put your demons to rest or resolve traumas that may have originated in your childhood or have been part of your life. There is a need to encourage each or both clients to discuss and, if possible, resolve any consistently troublesome problems or conflicts in their life before they proceed with marriage plans. All too often married couples come into marriage counseling when one of them complains about how he or she is expected to compensate for the neglect, abuse, or any number of other negative victimizations previously experienced by their partner. This need on the part of the victim often turns out to be a bottomless cup that can never be filled despite the Herculean efforts of their partner.

THE PANORAMIC VIEW
Who can or wants to think about bill paying, illness, dirty dishes, job layoffs, life insurance, pre-nuptial contracts, in-laws, etc. in the throes of passion or while gazing adoringly into the eyes of their lover? Yet, these are some of the very issues about which you may need to discuss your feelings and see the wisdom in exploring at the pre-marital stage. If you can do this without diminishing your desire for each other it will more than likely strengthen your resolve to marry.

LOVE IS BLIND
Before marriage, when you're "in love" there's no limit to sex, money, gifts, help, time or attention you are willing to share or bestow upon each other. Yet, more often than not, after marriage it's the absence of this very generosity that sends many couples into a tailspin, scurrying off to counseling or to the divorce courts. There is definitely some truth to the statement that love is blind. Whoever made it up should

have added, especially romantic love. However, love doesn't have to be blind and can remain just as strong if a couple is willing to look beyond those first flushes of self-induced enchantment. The decision and commitment to marry or just live together begs for a walk-through with a magnifying glass to see and explore beyond the mesmerizing effects of a couple's delight with each other.

In premarital counseling couples are encouraged to discuss their feelings about any issue, no matter how taboo, that they see as being problematic in their future.

SEXUAL ISSUES
Paul, 38, a CPA, and Donna, 41, an elementary school teacher, are examples of what at least one of them considered a hangup. They had been coming in for pre-marital counseling for two months. They were allowed to bring up each presenting issue in whatever order they found comfortable. I noted that we touched on where and how they were planning their future living arrangements, the sharing of household duties, bill paying, home décor and whatever else they felt was important. However, as we were winding down our sessions, I couldn't help but realize a glaring omission. There was no discussion about their feelings for each other or about their sex life. It seemed that whenever we got close to the subject they would veer off in another direction. It then occurred to me and my partner (who is male) that each of them might be more comfortable in one-on-one sessions. It was mutually agreed upon that they would each be seen individually for the next couple of meetings. Although Donna was considered a very competent, dedicated and enthusiastic teacher, for over fifteen years, her general manner was very self-effacing, ladylike and subdued. She was very soft-spoken and modest so we knew we had hit on the right formula when she appeared to be much more willing to talk about the intimate part of her life without Paul being present.

Donna related how Paul really went against type. She had not expected this straight-laced, punctilious accountant who was so publicly reserved and laid back to be as adventurous, inventive and vigorous a lover as he had turned out to be. His antics and explorations in the bedroom had at first surprised and turned her off. She acknowledged, however, that gradually he had tapped into a deep sensuality she had not heretofore realized she had or experienced. Although she felt she was still not functioning at Paul's level, she reluctantly admitted that she looked forward to their still infrequent sexual encounters. Her explanation for her not wishing to discuss their sex life was that she had come from a strict Catholic background. For her to acknowledge and discuss the flood gates Paul was beginning to open still seemed somewhat taboo to her since she was engaging in sex before marriage. Paul was very much aware of her background and how she felt about revealing any such intimacy to anyone. Out of concern for her feelings he had gone along with her reluctance to broach the subject in therapy.

Paul on the other hand found it very easy to share his sexual attitudes with my partner. He felt rather proud of himself because he was making a breakthrough in Donna's reserve by way of a great deal of patience and sensitivity to her feelings. He made it quite clear that the reward for his efforts had been well worth it. Once it was established that even though their attitudes towards and approach to sex may have been light years apart, their energy and desire for each other were pretty well matched. In this case, since opposites attract (as long as a couple agrees on the basics) this issue did not pose a roadblock. They appeared to be resolving their differences in this area. When they came back into sessions as a couple it was easier for them to discuss potential sexual problems such as sexual black mail, withholding sex, sexual rejections, jealousy, betrayal, and cheating and how any of these problems can derail a marriage. This, in turn led them to ways and means of spotting danger signals in advance and how to head them off at the pass or deal with them effectively before they got out of hand. It is not unusual for one member of a couple to figuratively swing from a chandelier, naked with his or her hair on fire while the other member, although by nature reserved and subdued, becomes quite willing and acquiescent. This does not mean that the partners are not sexually compatible. It only means that each one has a different modus operandi or means of self expression (Dharma and Greg come to mind). Compatibility lies in the amount of basic energy, drive and desire each participant has for the other and how evenly matched that is. There is no reason why this can't be expressed in any number of mutually acceptable ways. The bottom line is that the personal needs of each party are ultimately being met.

YOUR PLACE OR MINE
Another couple we dealt with was Norman, 45, head chef at a five-star restaurant, and Elyse 39, a producer of a cable television show. After a month of pre-marital counseling they appeared to have quickly resolved a lot of pre-nuptial and financial issues. They couldn't however, come to terms on where they would live. Norman had lived in his large garden apartment in an upscale suburban neighborhood for 22 years. He felt he had more than adequate space to accommodate the both of them. He was almost paranoid about living in midtown in the city. Elyse had a posh co-op on the East Side and had put a lot of time, energy and money into decorating it. She was, therefore, loathe to give it up. There did not appear to be a right or wrong choice here as much as a need for some type of compromise. Because they were both so strongly attached to their respective turfs we could only offer them alternative ways of thinking. The ultimate choice, of course, would be theirs.

Among some of the considerations or suggestions, the first of which another couple we had counseled was still carrying out, was that after marriage they each continue to live in and maintain their own apartments during weekdays. Since they both led such busy lives during the week, they could take turns spending weekends, days off, holidays and vacations at each other's place, which was pretty much what they were doing anyway. This way, neither of them would have to immediately disrupt or give up the comforts of their own home. It would not only be as though they were continuing to date but would give them time to change their minds at a later date. After much discussion they felt that this would not contribute to building a really solid marriage especially if Elyse became pregnant. After examining several other options they decided to find a third co-op they could both decorate which would reflect both their tastes, at the upper suburban end of Manhattan. They also opted to sublet their respective apartments on a temporary basis. They reasoned that in a worse case scenario, should the marriage hit a snag, they would each have a retreat to which they could return. It had been apparent all along that this possibility was the underlying cause of their initial reluctance to leave their own apartments in the first place.

HEAD OF THE HOUSEHOLD

Jill, 25, a beginning social worker, and Matthew, 26, who was working in a law firm and studying for the bar had been an item all through college. They came into counseling with no doubts about wanting to get married. Because they were quite young, they were surprised at the great number of issues they had not explored in depth before planning the final step. After four or five sessions they found themselves generally compatible with or could resolve their feelings about most of the issues discussed. Their sticking point was on how to handle the family finances. They had problems dealing with such things as bill payments, life insurance, emergency funds and how and by whom these should be handled. The most difficult of these to resolve was the payment of bills. Matthew's father had always given his mother an allowance to run the household but otherwise held all the family purse strings. Matthew felt that he should therefore be the main bread winner so they should use his checking account into which they would both deposit their paychecks so he could pay the bills. Jill on the other hand insisted on maintaining her own checking account and was all for her husband to be doing the same. They were finally helped to come to an agreement which allowed that each would keep their own personal checking accounts to use as they pleased but that they would also contribute an agreed upon amount of money to a third joint account. This account would pay for basics such as rent, food, utilities home furnishings and family emergencies. This was an account on which either of them could write a check for basic necessities in the event one of them were absent or became incapacitated.

NUTS AND BOLTS

Discussing differences of attitudes, opinions, feelings and learning how to compromise and negotiate the nuts and bolts of marriage at this stage of couplehood sets up a blue print of how to resolve any number of annoyances or future conflicts that are liable to surface after marriage. If a couple can amicably come to terms with their feelings and differences over what might be considered the vexations and harsh realities of marriage and still want to remain engaged or committed to each other, it's a definite plus for a more successful relationship after they say, "I do."

CHAPTER 3

Know Thyself

Instead of looking for the right mate, think in terms of becoming the right mate. Let's, for argument's sake, assume you are not in a relationship currently (even if you are). You would therefore be in a much better position to see yourself as you really are because your vision of yourself is not being obscured or identified by a current meaningful other's opinion of you. Whether you're male or female, your original sense of security and feelings of self esteem come from the way you were accepted and treated by your parents or caretakers during your childhood, or are possibly the results of therapy intervention during your adulthood. Parents who cannot deal with their own conflicts are generally unable to contribute positively to the emotional growth of their children. At some unconscious level, and sometimes consciously, their dysfunction is projected onto their child or children by way of inattention, the withholding of affection, verbal, physical or emotional abuse, rejection or abandonment. Anyone victimized by any of these destructive early life experiences or by consistent negative treatment (which more often than not can be just as traumatic) has a couple of strikes on them at the starting gate of the mating game.

Much has been said and written about the small child (at all different ages) that exists within all of us. If one's emotional development at any of these ages was arrested by such victimization, the results have been known to produce (which is not always immediately apparent) a frightened, needy, insecure, sometimes vindictive or psychopathic individual. Their self image is not only shaky but their real self is so submerged, they are often no longer in touch with their own behaviors and how it affects others.

It's difficult to deny the crucial role the dynamics of a family system plays in the maturation of the individual and how it will affect their future relationships. It's equally difficult not to recognize or make the connection between how each of us was raised and how that contributes (via concentric circles) to either peaceful, rational behavior or violent, war-like attitudes and how these two dynamics exist in the world side by side. Peace and war, like charity, begin at home. When one looks outside of male-female relationships, the family and the community and then moves onto the larger geographical picture one can understand Mahatma Ghandi's statement that peace between countries must rest on the solid foundation of love between individuals. Before one can truly love another, one must first accept, respect and love oneself.

SELF ESTEEM

There are two characteristics that are the sunshine and water of the adult persona. They are positive self esteem and emotional maturity. Self esteem has been deemed as positive self appraisal and acceptance and historically described (from a psychological point of view) as the ability of an adult to love or accept him or herself without the influence, assistance or suggestion of others. More recent studies repute this theory on the grounds that feelings of self worth emanate originally from our parents or caretakers during our growing up years. The internalization of this process translates into a continuing appreciation and need to be affirmed and accepted especially by meaningful others for the rest of our lives. When meaningful others, for whatever reason, treat us badly or negatively and no longer supply this appreciation or fulfill this need, those who hold themselves in high esteem will calculate the cost of maintaining such a relationship. If they deem the cost too high, they will thoughtfully consider or opt for greener fields or at least move away from what appears to have become a negative situation for them.

It appears, therefore that unaided or unsolicited good feelings about ourselves and sometimes enjoying and even needing the acceptance and approbation of meaningful others is a healthy balance or ideal in our system of self esteem. Nobody is going to feel good about themselves all the time but one should not throw out the baby with the bath water. The ability to realize how complicated liking and always accepting our own behavior on any consistent basis is a giant step toward understanding why we are not always going to like, accept or tolerate the conduct of our chosen partner or others who are meaningful to us.

EMOTIONAL MATURITY

The second desirable characteristic, emotional maturity, is a goal, it appears, that is never really reached. Realistically, we are all somewhere along its continuum in the process of getting there which means some of us are further along the path than others.

There are as many stages of maturity as there are stages of our lives—the hallmark of which appears to be the ability to deal with age appropriate challenges as they present themselves to us. Life is full of stress, both good and bad. Almost anyone can play a good hand. However, coping gracefully and productively with a bad one is much to be desired. The ability of one to use the past as a learning experience, the present in which to live and the future for which to plan, are all desirable elements of maturity without actually or necessarily making one mature. There are as many coping characteristics of human nature as there are circumstances that elicit them. It's difficult to say that any one or any combination of them is a definitive description of emotional maturity. Although we can always add to the following list of qualities that define a mature adult, these characteristics appear, by consensus of opinion, to top the list: a sense of humor about one's self as well as others, not taking one's self too seriously, the ability to identify with others via sympathy or empathy and to share their pain and joy, the ability to feel compassion for one's fellow man/woman, a willingness to listen, forgive and negotiate, the ability to be emotionally intimate and vulnerable without fear or loss of feelings of self, the ability to accept constructive criticism, the ability to know one's own tolerance limits if and when confronted with physical, emotional or psychological abuse or mistreatment as well as the ability to protect or defend oneself accordingly, the ability to maintain a balance between one's dependency needs and independence and the ability to recognize that the world is how you perceive it colored by your own background and conditioning and that the same is true of everyone else.

If all these character traits appear to be a bit much—and sound like a bid for sainthood, don't despair. Surprisingly most of us do have, to a greater or lesser degree most of these qualities. The rub is to what degree of each one. This is what makes emotional maturity such a complex state and why almost everyone is and can be located traveling somewhere along its path. We are, none of us, going to have all these aspects of our personality operating at their optimum level at all times. At anygiven time, depending on the circumstances, any of these qualities will surface—the point being here that we become aware of this dynamic and that the awareness hopefully raises our level of consciousness as to our need and capacity for expressing it.

EMOTIONAL DISGUISES

Getting to know oneself as well as also recognizing the possibility of a myriad of subterfuges under which everyone—at one time or another—may operate, is not necessarily an easy task. But maintaining pretenses and emotional disguises in the cold unremitting light of a marriage is truly a stressful and difficult if not impossible task.

In the therapeutic process, it becomes clear how the individual often lies or shades the truth about his or her real self (which in many cases they feel is not acceptable) or he or she is in a state of denial about what is obvious to everyone else. This is not necessarily done on purpose nor is it conspiratorial. The beliefs one has about oneself; more often than not, is arrived at through conditioning and a protective cover which not only hides the real person but also the painful source by which that self became that way. In helping an individual gain knowledge of him or herself, the therapist can sometimes tap into that source and bring the associated feelings out into the open thus freeing up the psychic energy that was fighting to hold it in place. Helping an individual thru negative memories and their resolution ultimately gives him or her some space and ability to make the informed choices of deciding if they then need to maintain their cloaking device or shed it. It's better for this to be dealt with within the privacy and security of a therapy session than by one's mate later on in a marriage. There it can be and often is construed in a negative or critical manner.

WHAT YOU NEED IN A MATE

Knowing your own emotional needs and how they can best be met is crucial not only to a marriage but also in your initial choice of a mate who hopefully will come closest to satisfying those needs. Keep in mind that your significant other is making his or her choice via the same criteria. It seems, therefore, reasonable to assume that you must not only choose the right mate. You must also be the right mate.

Everyone has their own way of going about finding what they believe they really want in a mate. There are those who go by their gut instinct and luckily arrive at their goal at least 80% of the time while others of a more analytic nature feel it's important to go so far as to literally list their criteria for a mate. A recent client, Joan, who was very practical as well as analytical, used a heading for each of her list of categories she felt were important for her mate to have. Her qualifications were so stringent that when she had completed her list even she had to acknowledge that she was seeking what we would consider a perfect person. It surprised her more to discover that her quest for perfection not only narrowed her chances of ever finding anyone vaguely suitable but, taken one step further, her need could be interpreted to also mean she didn't really want a serious relationship. She was then asked what percent of the qualities she had listed would satisfy her based on zero to 100%. We settled on 85%. Comparing her first list with other female clients, I found their acceptance percentage choices ranged from 60% to 90% of what they would be willing to settle for in a mate.

Let's back pedal for a moment and take a look at the category headings under which my client placed her qualities in the order that she presented them. Physical appearance, personality, health, hygiene, character, life style, finances, social consciousness, compatibility, profession. After being in therapy for six months, Joan gradually began to realize she was choosing or allowing herself to be chosen by men, many of whom only superficially reflected some, if any, of her listed qualities. She also became aware of why she had so many aborted relationships which often involved her need to endow her partners with what she was seeking even though they clearly did not possess them.

TRYING TO CHANGE SOMEONE
She was helped to see how she also attempted to influence her partners to aspire to her level of perfection. This in turn led her to understand that anyone with whom she decided to mate would have to have already had many of the qualities she was seeking, on their own. She learned the hard way that if a person is not what you want them to be or doesn't possess qualities that are important or meaningful to you, you cannot change, influence or force them to your way of thinking. Even when you believe that your idea of what their behavior should be is to their advantage, or "right," they will in all likelihood balk at your efforts to change them. Most people will sense that inherent in your suggestion or persuasion for such change is a criticism of who and what they already are.

Really knowing yourself means you are capable of thinking twice before jumping into a committed relationship such as live-in partners or marriage, especially during the throes of infatuation, physical attraction or sexual passion. Most people, especially men, feel that if you are willing to marry them you have pretty much accepted them the way they are and will see no need to change themselves afterwards. They will, therefore often take any demands or suggestions for change in their behavior or life style not only as personal criticism but also as a form of deception on your part in that you did not voice these complaints or distractions before marriage. It, therefore, becomes each partner's priority to learn to read the handwriting on the wall much more clearly—not so much about your mate's m.o. but about your own present and future reaction to it. Their behavior will, in all probability, continue any way—longer than you will care to tolerate it. This is all part of getting to know what you are willing to live with in the future.

RESPONSIBILITY FOR OUR OWN FEELINGS

It's a real downer when your partner doesn't live up to your expectations, cannot be depended or relied upon or is not there for you when you need him or her. Our initial reaction to any of these occurrences is one of anger or outrage at our partner even when or if we don't show it or discuss it.

However, if we view this state of affairs thru the right end of the telescope, we might become reluctantly aware of the fact that it is ourselves with whom we are disappointed or angry because we chose the mate or allowed ourselves to be chosen by him or her. Unfortunately each of us is responsible for his or her own feelings. The hurt, anger and frustration you feel is seldom experienced by your mate who is often oblivious to what you are going through. You are the one whose entrails are in an uproar. Your mate will often go blithely on his or her way until you bring your angst to their attention. Unfortunately, because it is second hand to them you will be lucky to get an attentive ear or an off hand acknowledgment or apology. Because most people don't care for the discomfort inherent in confrontation, they may even resent you for instigating it and become uncommunicative until the storm blows over. In any case, you may often be left holding an emotional bag that takes more time than you care to spend to get rid of it. You need to know yourself well enough to not only be able to predict your own reactions and feelings in certain negative situations but also remain in control of them. Self knowledge is worth the effort if for no other reason than that it will reduce the intensity of the hurt, anger or pain you are bound to feel in certain adverse circumstances. This, in turn, will at least keep your head clearer as to how best to function to your own advantage.

SAVING PSYCHIC ENERGY

The pursuit of knowing oneself, although a simplistic statement, is a life long project. Such knowledge not only involves a conscious awareness of self but also has to take into consideration the way meaningful others (who can be more objective) see us. We generally believe we are on pretty familiar terms with ourselves, when in fact, most of us have to go through several life experiences, both positive and negative, before learning how we will really feel, act, or react by the time we come out on the other side of these experiences. In relationships, the trick is in knowing yourself so well, you can, with fair accuracy, predict how you are going to feel, act or react in the instance of a mate's negative or positive behavior. The emphasis here is on your reaction which is all you can change, not your mate's behavior. The art of this kind of prediction has something to do with studying in retrospect and really learning your own behavior after each experience, especially a negative one. This is not easy in the midst of emotional outrage but it is preferable to losing it and having to back track later. It is also preferable to using up your psychic energy in anger, hurt feelings, recriminations, spite or revenge.

THE KEY TO ENLIGHTENED SELF INTEREST
An once of prevention.... look before you leap. etc., are trite but they are good starting points on any emotional venture. They are the beginnings of consequential thinking. Simply put, any action you are planning to take behooves you to seriously consider its pros and cons. Everything contains its own opposite. No matter how unlikely it seems, the opposite might occur. This acknowledgment alone takes the sting out of a lot of nasty surprises. The ability to be aware of the outcome of any of your own feelings, actions, or behavior is the cornerstone of self-awareness. The ability to satisfy or make others comfortable or at least do no harm to them in your pursuit of arranging you affairs to your own advantage is the key to enlightened self interest. You will often find it difficult to ascertain the motivation or the rationale for other's behavior even if you are very much in touch with your own. Even then, you may not be able to make an emotional connection to them, but you will be able to acknowledge and accept, as well as control, you reaction to it.

WHERE TO START
Aside from the school of hard knocks, otherwise termed as experience, how does one get to know one's self well? There are personal as well as professional methods. On your own, keeping a diary of not only the meaningful events in your life over a protracted period of time,

but also recording your feelings and reactions to these events is a good start. If possible, conversations with parents or original caretakers (if they are still around and you are on speaking terms) about pockets of your childhood and how you reacted to the way you were treated can often be very revealing. You may still be curious about or have dreams, sometimes disturbing, which disrupt your usual productive flow. The amount of truth you glean from these methods will give you clues germane to your behavior and personality. Keep in mind that if your parents gave you a positive image of yourself for at least the first 16-18 years of your life, you will not find it necessary to seek or define your identity or sense of self through the approval and acceptance of strangers.

On a professional level, you would probably go pretty much through the same process, using your own memory with the help of an objective, supportive therapist. Such intervention can be particularly advantageous in the case of emotionally blocked areas and other rough spots you might find difficult to retrace or handle alone. This process, if nothing else, teaches us that as adults we all bring some emotional garbage into our adult relationships. When we don't take the time and effort to examine what we are accumulating, we begin to stockpile it. Then we have to use up a lot of psychic energy to keep it in place so that it doesn't spill over into our daily functioning. Consequently, anyone under a great deal of stress or living in pressure cooker conditions learns the toll this can also take on their physical body. Often there is a tendency to bring the ensuing conflict into our relationship with a significant other, unconsciously. Unfortunately we sometimes mistakenly believe that our dilemma will somehow be relieved or resolved through the object of our affections.

It makes sense therefore to lighten that load before we begin an affair, if possible, and definitely before getting into a committed relationship. Hopefully, we will then have more psychic energy to pour into dealing with our chosen partner in the art of making him or her happy rather than unloading our emotional junk on them.

CHAPTER 4

Your Emotional Health

Shortly after an infant or very young child learns to say "Mama", "Dadda" and make a few monosyllabic demands, he or she learns to say "no" loudly and clearly as any mother will attest to who has experienced the "terrible two's". Since most behavior is learned from the parents it's not long thereafter that the child experiences, via either parent, additional negatives such as, "stop", "don't", "no, no", "that's bad", "that's dirty"' that's not nice", or "mother and daddy won't love you", all of which are negative verbalizations designed to force the child to conform and to seek their approval. Depending on the manner and atmosphere in which such dictums are delivered, the child to one degree or another incorporates certain feelings about him or herself that can last for a lifetime. In those cases where a great deal of this negative programming is closely followed by or simultaneously reinforced with physical punishment (depending upon the general emotional environment in which it is dispensed) such doubly negative treatment can and often does leave lasting emotional scars on a growing child.

There's a child in all adults but no adult in the child except potentially. Parents or parent figures often make the mistake of too quickly weighting a child down with their own adult neuroses in the form of inordinate demands, attitudes, anxieties and mores without realizing that the child simply hasn't lived as long as they have or hasn't had enough life experience or time for the readiness needed to accept the next plateau or stage of social behavior. In many cases, children may still be battling, emotionally, previously unresolved victimizations that occurred at an earlier stage of their development which continue to get in the way of them mastering what is currently being expected of them. Imagine what kind of effect this has upon the growing child if and when they begin to realize how untenable and irrational such demands were or are and how their feelings as little people were never taken into consideration.

Adults emerging from this kind of parenting can, and often do, spend years feeling resentment and hostility against those they might most want to attract. Instead they constantly alienate them, in their attempt at solving the postnatal or authority figure situations that existed when they were younger. Although we may be unconscious as to the origins of our feelings of discomfort with or the lack of acceptance of ourselves, we certainly know, at least externally, when things are not going well for us. We may notice that we don't seem to be able to get along or ahead financially, romantically or socially—at least not the way we'd like to.

PSYCHOSOMATIC ILLNESS

Which of us at some time or other in our lives hasn't therefore wondered about our own emotional state of affairs? We may not have used that terminology but it certainly isn't uncommon that we may have asked ourselves questions like, "Why can't I be successful at getting what I want?" "Why do I keep doing the same stupid thing over and over again?" or "Was I crazy to do a thing like that?" or "Why can't I stand up for my own rights?" It's also a pretty rare individual who hasn't at one time or another felt some form of anxiety, stress or depression that can loosely be put into the categories of temporary, mild, periodic, pervasive or chronic. And for those of us who don't recognizably fall into any of the above categories, we may be suffering from emotional problems that manifest themselves in the form of such physical ailments as migraine headaches, ulcers, intestinal disorders, skin rashes, asthma, etc. Such aliments are commonly referred to as psychosomatic illnesses. In some cases some neurological disorders such as multiple sclerosis or brain tumors have been diagnosed as being the result of an emotional or behavioral disturbance. Even cancer has now come under the scrutiny of the psychologists and the psychiatrist. They are finding clues that point to unresolved stress, tension and/or anxiety as often being factors that lead to or aggravate cancer in patients.

DOUBTS ABOUT YOURSELF
Our usual approach to dealing with psychological problems is not one of actually sitting down and taking inventory of our state of mental health. Rather, there is a tendency, to wait until feelings overwhelm us and then ask ourselves, do we need professional help and that question alone has been known to trigger all sorts of anxieties. Actually, if you are well enough to have some doubts about yourself, you're better off than some one who refuses to admit something is wrong with themselves even though it's obvious to almost everyone else that that person's life is in shambles. If you find you are contemplating the question over a prolonged period of time or in depth, that very concern gives you the answer that you might probably benefit from ventilating or expressing you inner feelings to a trusted friend, minister or professional in the field. You would do no less than visit a medical doctor if you had a recurring cough or persistent pain in your chest. Almost any severe physical discomfort would undoubtedly send you scurrying off to a medical specialist in a hurry.

The science that deals with emotional health under the catchall name of Psychology is still not only relatively new but also inexact, varied, and as tenuous as the multitude of environments, cultures, past experiences and personalities to which it must address itself. Therapy or professional help in this area is still considered by many to be a closet situation. Psychotherapy has only recently (in the past 40 to 50 years) emerged as a workable haven for functioning people plagued by neuroses as well as for the psychologically non-functioning. The desire to know whether or not one is emotionally intact usually takes precedence over how one feels generally on a day to day basis, give or take the occasional wide swing of circumstances that occur to us. How you feel is still really the best barometer of your own emotional health.

MENTAL HEALTH CHECK-UP

What does not occur to most people is that a mental health check-up or short term therapy used as crisis intervention need be no more taxing or terrifying than a physical check-up. One is certainly as important as the other since human beings operate as a whole unit. The psyche and soma are interdependent upon the successful operation of each for the other. It should also be noted that a visit to a well-chosen therapist does not constitute life long commitment or for that matter, even a protracted period of time. The amount of time you spend with professional help has much to do with the longevity and severity of your problem coupled with the resistance you put up during the therapy process as well as the intensity of the desire on your part to be relieved of your symptoms or problems. This, of course, differs in each therapeutic situation and with each individual.

Short of considering professional help, how do we ascertain the state of our emotional health and what can we do about it? On a scale of one to ten if you have been rating yourself on the down side of five in physical appearance, physical health, physical surroundings and your workaday world, it should serve as a guide and some consciousness raising to you that all is not well on the inside.

If you would be willing to honestly assess the degree to which the following needs have been met during your maturation years you might be able to match them up to the feelings you have about yourself today. There are certain emotional needs that are essential to all human beings and have been from the day they were born and will continue to be until the day they die. Almost any prolonged state of emotional health can be measured by the presence, absence or degree to which human beings have experienced the following:

EMOTIONAL NEEDS

LOVE For almost everyone this tops the list. In its many facets, variations and interpretations it holds as many meanings for humans at different phases and stages of their life as there are humans. For the sake of brevity, let us say that at the pre-adult level it should be to a great extent, unconditional parental acceptance, warm and touching, tempered with understanding, guidance and fair and consistent discipline. At the adult level, assuming the pre-adult has experienced such acceptance, it is the ability to give to another human being the ultimate in warm, physical, emotional and personal contact coupled with a genuine selfish need to receive the same in return from the object or objects of their affection.

SECURITY This needs to be experienced physically and emotionally from birth. If a sense of security is generally maintained for the growing child for at least the first 16 years of his or her life, it opts for a fair degree of emotional health in adulthood. It's just as possible to experience this feeling, in a one-parent household, as it is where there are two parents, or in adoptive or guardian situations. It's not who creates the atmosphere but the quality of the atmosphere created.

ACCEPTANCE Once you have arrived chronologically at adulthood and presuming you have been fortunate enough to experience a satisfactory amount of love and security, it is still tremendously important that you feel accepted by your peers and other meaningful people in your life. This becomes a lot easier if your parental conditioning taught you how to accept yourself and how well you can realistically appraise the negatives and positives in your life. This last benefit is easily discerned by how often and how well you avoid the former (negatives) and how accepting you are of the latter (positives). There are several sub-headings under each of these broad categories of human emotional need, which qualify and clarify the ingredients that supply such needs.

Under the feeling of love should have come the guidance you received where hopefully you were given a foundation for making the choices of your personal value system and beliefs. In a world whose mores, manners and life styles have been changing with such lightning speed over the past 50 years, this is a difficult task at best. What your parent figures did (by example) was always much louder than what they said and had much more influence on your adult behavior.

Under the feeling of security should have come discipline, which in any form needed to be firm, consistent, fair and rational in order to give you a sense of order and the feeling of concern shown for your welfare. So called "good" behavior should always have been noticed, recognized and rewarded, at least emotionally.

Under the feeling of acceptance should have come the need for sharing. This sharing should have included everything from the facts of life to whatever is going on intimately in the family. Since occasions of death, divorce, financial setbacks, illness or other family reverses (as well as happy events) occur in all human families, why would one not share, in as tactful and loving a way as possible, the reality of these situations with our little humans to the extent that they question or can understand them? How else would you be equipped to cope adequately with such happenstance as you yourselves grew into adulthood?

Emotional needs that apply to children do not differ as one grows older. They only take different forms. There's no such thing as reaching maturity as though it were some stage or plateau that we are all bound to get to or a brass ring that is finally caught. We do reach a physical peak in maturing but it doesn't mean we stop growing physically. It only means that we continue to grow (or change which is what growth is) in different directions. Emotionally we also continue to grow (or should) until we die. We are always in the process of maturing by means of trial and error. If we are going in what seems to be the right direction for us we should be noticing that we are experiencing less error or at least we should be coping better with or living more comfortably with our own choices.

Basic emotional needs follow us into old age. The curiosity or love of learning, the desire to survive the vicissitudes of life that surround us, the need to make and sustain friendships and the need to trust and share with another human being are with us always.

It is, of course, highly possible to have had an emotionally satisfying upbringing and still experience from mild to severe emotional upsets. It doesn't mean that you need to head for a rubber room. It means you may be at a crossroads, or in an unfamiliar dilemma and don't believe you can trust your feelings and therefore may need to step back from your problem to view as objectively as possible what is really going on with yourself at that moment. The most self-confident people in the world go through such crises. Part of their self-confidence grew out of the fact that sooner or later they were able to recognize and deal with their dilemma for what it was rather than allow it to panic them into unreasonable, unproductive, destructive or negative behavior. Anyone can play a good hand. It is one of the tests of maturity to be able to cope successfully with the adversity that often comes in the form of a lousy hand.

There is no composite test or quiz that will give you satisfactory or absolute answers as to your own inner emotional environment. Such devices can turn out to be intellectual traps unless the knowledge gained is coupled with one's own personal feelings, which are the best barometer we have to measure comfort or discomfort with our inner selves.

DANGER SIGNS
One of the greatest difficulties experienced by people who are emotionally out of it is acknowledging that they have a problem. Some of the signs to pay attention to (and consider seeking help for) especially if such signs are prolonged, constant or intense in nature are:

1. An inability to make even small decisions.
2. Chronic or pervasive depression or regular bouts with the "blues".
3. On-going feelings of living in a gray area where everything and everybody seem meaningless to you often accompanied by thoughts of suicide.
4. Constant irritability, feelings of frustration and nervousness where the slightest noise, utterance by another or disagreement sets you off.
5. Self-destructive behavior you often feel guilty about later (double stress) and keep telling yourself you will correct but never do, such as promiscuity, overindulgence in drinking, gambling, exposure to danger, eating, or substance abuse.
6. Being accident prone to the extent of frequently seriously injuring yourself.
7. Constant feelings of hostility, anger or need for revenge or retaliation or the taking out of such resentment not only against authority figures or peers but also against children, pets or live things that are helpless, less strong or that are dependent upon you.

8 Frequent suffering from chronic colds, bouts of asthma, ulcers, colitis, migraine headaches, skin rashes or any number of other physically debilitating disorders not contagious, hereditary or congenital in nature.

9 Incapacitating phobias about such things as heights, space, water, animals, planes, elevators, small areas of space, etc. Compulsive behavior such as counting cement cracks when walking, repeated hand washing, the constant checking of one's surroundings for safety, etc.

10 Overwhelming fears that someone, or everyone, something or everything or some public institution is out to get you, do you harm or take something away from you when there is no basis in fact for this fear.

11 Frequent sexual and marital difficulties, inability to perform sexually, to love another person, make or sustain friendship or a relationship or make an emotional commitment even when you believe you would really like to.

12 Inability to get over a disappointment, the loss of a loved one, loss of a treasured object or pet or consistent failure to attain a certain goal.

13 Fear or dislike of ever being alone or spending creative time with yourself. Constant need for companionship or the company of others regardless of who they are.

TIME OUT

It helps to realize that regardless of how consciously unaware we may be of it, we are all bombarded by hostile as well as pleasant stimuli during our waking hours. It is only a chosen few, (if any) who manage to avoid the hassles of every day living. When our defense mechanisms are no longer working against the negative forces, it is then that emotional upheaval and illness occurs. It's not a bad idea to proclaim a "Stop the World I Want to Get Off" day to check how well our defenses are working since the healthiest among us are subject to stress on a daily basis. Stress, of course, can be positive (as a prodder or influence to survive, succeed, or do better)—or negative (as an agent causing our mental and physical apparatus to collapse or subside in the face of formidable odds). Stress is, therefore, different things to different people. What might constitute tension, fear, anxiety, depression, insomnia or ulcers in one person might be merely an impetus to go on to bigger and better things in another. Knowing your stress quotient (based on past experience) should add more to your self knowledge, thereby giving you a guideline as to what to tackle, what to avoid, when and wherever possible, and when to seek relief from either. Keep in mind that even if you don't feel mental stress (because sometimes it's too painful for the mind to deal with) the body has a way of taking on what the mind often won't deal with. Hostile stimuli combined with the stress of trying to cope are often the cause of colds, headaches, migraines, ulcers, colitis, heart disease, arthritis, skin disorders or rashes and according to most recent studies, cancer. None of these ailments are contagious or necessarily hereditary. They are more often than not results of thwarted attempts to deal with constant frustration or a lowered resistance to stress.

SELF EVALUATION

Check the following list (many of which cannot be avoided) on a scale of one to ten as to how much stress you believe you would feel or have already felt in each of the following situations. When you find yourself going over five in any of these areas you should become very aware of and circumspect about learning how to deal with such situations (if possible before they occur) to your own advantage even if it means seeking the help of a professional—temporarily. A good rule of thumb as to when this type of action is feasible is to carefully weigh the time and energy spent trying to deal with your unwanted stress alone and consider the price this constitutes. Such a price often depletes the time and psychic energy we all need to function productively as well as be at peace, feel reasonably happy and be able to respond comfortably to the atmosphere around us. Sometimes such help prods us into perhaps considering an alternative life style that more suitably fits our emotional make up.

STRESS TEST

Below are 30 stress producing situations which can be both positive and negative. On a scale of one to ten, write the number with a plus (+) if it's positive or a minus (-) if it's negative illustrating the strength of the stress as you believe it would, will or has affected you.

1. Death of a lover or a spouse _____
2. Separation or divorce _____
3. Imprisonment (or any limitations on your freedom of movement) _____
4. Death of a close family member or friend _____
5. Severe injury or illness. _____
6. Getting married. _____
7. Having your first love affair _____
8. Sexual hang-ups. _____
9. Pregnancy _____
10. Losing your job _____
11. Financial reverse _____
12. Losing your home or apartment (eviction, fire, etc.) _____
13. Moving _____
14. Going on vacation _____
15. Returning from vacation _____
16. Job related unhappiness _____
17. Not being recognized for true worth (job, friends, and family). _____
18. Series of aborted love affairs _____
19. Abortion _____
20. Student problems _____
21. (failing, pressure, boredom, etc.) _____
22. Family personality clashes _____
23. In-law problems _____
24. Marriage or live-in non-communication _____
25. Children—non-communication _____
26. Recurring dreams or nightmares _____
27. Being unmarried or stereotyped as a single _____

28 Racial discrimination   _____
29 Daily barrage of reports from news media   _____
30 Feelings of inferiority   _____
31 Loneliness (which can occur whether   _____
you are married or single).

There is something to making affirmations, try repeating to yourself as often as possible:

My thoughts and my feelings are mine alone. They are neither good nor bad, they just are, and I'm allowed to have them. I choose to make them as positive for myself as I can.

CHAPTER 5

The Dance of Males and Females

Because there is an emotional gap (which, hopefully, is diminishing in the socialization process of males and females today) as well as a biological one, a lot of differences in the two genders' perception and points of view are unavoidable. The big Kahuna is the communication gap. It is not enough to know that it exists but also to understand why.

A recent brain scan test by Dr. Jenny Harasty, a lecturer at the school of Communication Disorder in Sydney, Australia discovered that two language control areas in the female brain are significantly larger than those of the male. Thus women come already well equipped in the socialization process. After measuring the brain of an equal number of men and women after death, Dr. Harasty found that the Wernke center, which helps us interpret words and sounds takes up 30% more space in women's brains than in men's. She also discovered that the Broca area, which helps us select words, sentences and grammatical connections, is 20% larger in women than in men. This biological difference is a significant finding because the scientists involved believe these differences are probably due to a combination of genetic programming and the fact that the female brain develops more rapidly during childhood. They also concluded that women getting angry or frustrated with men who are, or become silent and uncommunicative, need to know that it's not necessarily men's fault. They often can't respond as rapidly or put their thoughts into words as quickly as women can. It would go a long way towards building the bridge of communication between men and women if women would be more patient and give their men more time and understanding when they are talking. Who knows, it might not only help men to share their thoughts more often and more clearly, but also render them more favorably disposed to their mate just for this tolerance.

MALE & FEMALE ROLE MODELS
In working with dysfunctional families as well as doing pre-marital counseling, it became necessary to investigate why married couples were attracted to each other in the first place. An exploration of this dynamic revealed that (and this is particularly true in single parent homes or wherever there is only an intermittent or absentee father) both males and females more often than not unconsciously choose partners who have similar value systems, attitudes, behaviors, beliefs and characters and sometimes even physical characteristics of the mother. This is because mothers are more consistently in the household, more "there" for their children and have most of the care-taking responsibilities. Mothers cannot be role model for their sons, they can only love, nurture and be there for them. To the extent the young male experiences this, it will have an impact upon his choice and treatment of a female when he becomes an adult. If there is a father in the home, the interaction between his father and mother will dictate their son's attitude and behavior towards the female or females of his choice. In the case of the female, since there is usually a mother or female caretaker in presence, the daughter has a built-in role model, whose characteristics she will incorporate without necessarily being aware of it. Because there are many families without a father or father figure, and even when there is a father, if he is a non-participating or only an intermittent one, his daughters often grow up experiencing the male as an enigma. Many young women have had poor father-daughter relationships, devoid of feelings of protection, respect, trust and unconditional acceptance. A worse scenario is if at one time they were daddy's little girl or if he was only around in their single digit years. His subsequent absence became even more devastating to them as they grew into young womanhood. Girls often get their ideas of what a man should be from the movies,

television, romance novels and other media sources which give them a distorted unrealistic or romantic view of what they believe or need to believe men are. It's no wonder women are so often accused of men-bashing whether it's deserved or not. It's rational to assume that they need some kind of outlet for their frustration at having their illusions constantly crushed.

ABSENT MALES

Young women who don't grow up in a household where there was a constant, dependable, caring, concerned father have to create such an image out of whole cloth for themselves and try to match it in the mating game. Unfortunately, the success of this endeavor is so rare they more often than not end up endowing some undeserving male with these sought after qualities. This frequently and ultimately turns out to be frustrating, unproductive and disappointing leaving these young women even more disillusioned depressed or bitter without understanding how to extricate themselves from their pattern of choices.

MEN BETTER EQUIPPED TO CHOOSE

On the other hand, males, who have been consistently exposed, however positively or negatively, to their mother's characteristics, have a tremendous advantage over their female counterparts. They get to know early on how to maneuver and manipulate their mothers for what they want or need—not necessarily in a negative sense. They at least learn about and are subject to the female psyche replete with moods, outlook, value system etc, at a much greater depth than do their sisters with their fathers. Whether mother was a foreboding presence or a loving benign one, because of her ever presence (or possible absence) it will have a great impact upon how the male relates to females when he becomes an adult. He is, after all, armed (at an unconscious level) with much more information about females. This does not mean that males will make better choices than females in choosing a mate. It only means that males are probably more in touch at a subconscious level with what they really want or don't want in a female. By sheer numbers, considering the ratio of men to women, they are statistically in a better position to pick and choose to get what they want (even if the choice turns out to be a really bad one).

It seems that even though women, in may cases, grow up without an acceptable father-figure—which contributes to their inability to know what the male psyche is really about, today's woman, more than ever before is into investigating, exploring and finding out, through whatever means necessary, how close she can come to a suitable mate before taking the proverbial plunge.

There are, of course, many aspects of the male psyche and personality that daughters may never become aware of in association with their fathers. By the time these men have become presumably good fathers of growing children as adolescents, their attitudes and behavior with relation to the opposite sex will generally be somewhat different from that of their daughters' young suitors.

PRECONDITIONS

Women in general, need to feel they are wanted, respected and cared about and loved before engaging in sexual contact with a man. They also need to have fairly strong feelings for the person with whom they decide to share themselves. There are of course exceptions to this rule. But even when women engage in sexual behavior without these needs or feelings, unless they are nymphomaniacs (if there is such a thing) prostitutes or sociopaths, they will readily attempt to find excuses or rationale for their behavior out of guilt shame, embarrassment or bravado. Men, on the other hand, do not need to have any deep emotional reasons for expressing themselves sexually. And it is not unusual for them to declare that they do have such feelings (knowing how the female psyche works) in order to obtain sexual gratification from a female. Wherein it appears that orgasms for women are generally an overall body spreading sensation male orgasms are fairly local and can more easily be achieved in any number of ways. The mere picture of or physical attraction to a female is enough to interest a male in desiring sexual intercourse with her. He does not view one night stands or non-call backs with the same concerns as women and is very good at using all the ploys and pronouncements necessary to convince a female to sleep with him.

This is so inherent in men's nature or conditioning that it is not a characteristic so much to be changed (although most females will disagree with this) as it is to be understood by women so they can behave and or react accordingly in their own best interests.

MARRIED LIFE TODAY

The difference between men and women are never ending especially when one considers the access we all have to so much more information today which impacts upon our most important discussions. Family traditions, routines and life styles are, as we speak, drastically changing, being re-arranged, destroyed or shattered on a daily basis. This leaves today's couples to make up their own scenarios of what married life should be as well as an internal support system upon which to rely that will hopefully help them solve their problems. Getting members of a couple to see, hear, experience and mirror the feelings of each other promotes the art of communication between them. It also helps remove the filters of emotional arousal based on cultural beliefs, primal fears, ethnic beliefs, internalized old wives' tales and unexplained anxieties. One of the results of this art is that it slows down the preparation of a rebuttal before each has thoroughly listened to and explored what is being said by the other—thus enabling couples to struggle thru the language barrier of words that heretofore have been translated differently by each sex. In learning how to decode each other's buzz words, a couple is half way to understanding that the task before them is not so much about changing the behavior of their mate as it is understanding it. At that juncture, it is then easier to accept or tolerate the idiosyncrasies or attitudes of one's partner and sustain the relationship—as long as the behavior does not really cause physical or emotional harm or hardship to the other partner. However, a partner who feels truly damaged has to be able to express how they feel about this in the hopes that he or she will get his or her message across. The results of this exchange can and often does determine the health and longevity of the relationship.

INTIMACY

One of the biggest differences between males and females is their perception of and the way they handle intimacy. Men tend to view intimacy as being associated with sexual activity where to a large extent they can be very powerful or very vulnerable. A man's idea of letting his emotional guard down or being in a position where he might be considered unmanly is so devastating to him he is generally not too keen on adding to his vulnerability by revealing or sharing things about himself for which he might be viewed unfavorably or which might elicit criticism. Women on the other hand, in search of acceptance, consideration, caring and understanding sometimes go overboard with a revelation of themselves (because of their fear of alienation) in an effort to bond more securely with their mate. Half the essence of intimacy is the ability to reveal and share odd, unusual or personal histories and traits with one's mate respectively. The other half of intimacy is the ability of the other mate to accept or understand these traits or histories without condemnation or criticism as being part and parcel of his or her mate's persona.

FORESTALLING ABUSE

If this ritual is not practiced and does not become resolved as well as a part of the relationship before marriage it will be extremely difficult to initiate after marriage where one is more likely to feel in trapped circumstances. Really understanding and learning how to be empathetic or at least sympathetic with one's mate goes a long way towards preventing verbal, emotional and especially physical abuse on the part of either partner (which is unthinkable) particularly against women and children. In any situation, violence of any sort is not a solution. The propensity of either partner to resort to physical abuse needs to be investigated explored and resolved immediately at the beginning level of a relationship and definitely before marriage.

CHAPTER 6

The Dynamics of Couple Therapy

The process of dealing with pre-marital or otherwise committed couples is quite similar to that of dealing with already married couples. The exception is that with married couples the damage is already done and the step has already been taken from which one or both members may or may not wish or be able to extricate themselves. This latter situation is, of course, more complicated and sometimes gets pretty hairy especially if there are children involved.

In pre-marital counseling couples have the option of withdrawing from a relationship with a minimum of jagged edges (assuming there are no children involved). There is still the opportunity for them to arrive at the conclusion that they are not compatible or meant for each other.

The ensuing situations generally suggest different observations:

TWO SCENARIOS
1 One member of a couple is generally uncooperative and balks at the idea of pre-marital counseling and their attitude is one of emotional withdrawal from couplehood if they feel pressured to participate in counseling. The other member is very much in favor of pre-marital counseling and doesn't feel entirely comfortable or ready to jump into the final frontier without it.
OBSERVATIONS: The chances of survival for these two as a couple exist but they are poor because the participants are not mutually interested in a very basic dynamic that is essential to a relationship. Both members

need to be willing to discover whatever they can about each other. This may also be a clue that they probably don't share other basic beliefs or mutual interests.

2 Both partners appear to be attracted to and reasonably happy with each other and genuinely interested in counseling before marriage but have some reservations about their ability to be there for each other over the long haul or just want to reinforce what they already believe.
OBSERVATION: If this couple is strong in at least three of the following categories of their relationship they have a pretty good chance of surviving. 1) They have much in common, some similar interests, are good friends and share similar ideas about finances, life style etc. 2) They fulfill each other's emotional needs, generally trust and accept each other with few reservations. 3) There is a mutually strong physical and sexual attraction and bond between them. 4) They share the same beliefs about having and raising children.

The understanding this couple can gain from pre-marital counseling (depending upon to what degree each of the above categories are shared by them) appears to be considerable and bodes well for a favorable future).

Every therapist has his or her own methodology of dealing with clients. Each client is an individual and rarely fits any particular mold or model possibly preconceived by the therapist which hopefully the therapist has learned to discard through trial and error. The awareness of strategies and solutions that don't work is paramount in the give and take that occurs during treatment. A good therapist is constantly seeking and researching new methods that work for each individual with whom he or she comes in contact.

DEALING WITH THE INDIVIDUALS BEFORE THE COUPLE
Helping the client get in touch with and know himself or herself as the individual he or she was before being a part of a couple is of prime importance. People who do not know themselves well will find it difficult to understand how they are perceived by others. Also, if one enters a committed relationship and in the process loses a sense of self

or if when things begin to unravel emotionally, he or she will find it almost impossible to return to the person they were—who is—in the long run the one that will have to pick up the pieces.

Rational people know who they are from a physical, mental, material and situational point of view. They also know something about their emotional make-up. But there are blind spots in all of us that prevent us from acknowledging or being aware of some of our emotional garbage or the "why" we behave as we do. Until we can not only accept our own behavior but also be aware of how it is perceived by and affects others—we cannot make any changes in it, or make informed choices as to how to proceed with our lives. The need to deal with each individual separately, when dealing with couples, for whatever time it takes for that client to really be in touch with himself or herself, precedes dealing with the clients as a couple. The amount of time spent on this journey of self exploration will differ with each person. It is generally determined by both clients themselves when they are ready to be seen as a couple. This will not necessarily remain a static situation. In a client-centered atmosphere, from time to time, each of these individuals can still be seen alone, should the occasion arise, or if the client should make such a request.

Why see each member of a couple separately? Almost everyone of us has experienced a first love, sometimes intensely, or several loves or infatuations thereafter and we believe the experience to be different for us, each time it happens. That usually depends upon where we are on the emotional maturation scale.

CASE HISTORY

Let's use Laura and Dylan as examples, who came to couples therapy believing they were madly in love with each other and were only in pre-marital counseling because their minister had recommended it. They wanted him to be cognizant of the fact that they had taken his advice and that they had at least showed up for a few sessions. At first, they did not appear to take seriously any of the testing sessions or questions related to what had attracted each of them to the other and appeared to go along with the program only because it was expected of them.

When they were separated and dealt with individually my partner, who is a male, worked with Dylan while I worked with Laura. She dreamily related all the romantic encounters she and Dylan had shared and ended one of her narrations with and her exact words were "I don't think I really lived or existed before I met Dylan."

RED FLAG

For this therapist that statement was a red flag. This young woman was 37 years old, had never been married but had had numerous affairs and relationships the longest of which had lasted 6 months. Her partner Dylan, 36, was twice divorced. When asked might there have been some other reason she was willing to seek premarital counseling since the minister's recommendation appeared to be only part of it, Laura reluctantly explained how, having been in numerous previous relationships that had not worked out, she felt that men in general were not always what they purported themselves to be. As she warmed up to the subject she went on to say that ultimately in all her liaisons, these men had either left her shortly after sexual encounters, turned out to be commitment phobic, were generally unreliable, emotionally unavailable or were just simply self absorbed sleaze balls. She went on to iterate that this time she really did not want to make another mistake and felt it wouldn't hurt to know a little more about Dylan than she did in order not to have to suffer through yet another disappointment. She acknowledged that she was the one who had initiated the idea of pre-marital counseling in which he had definitely been reluctant to become involved.

By now there was more than one red flag. The fact that she needed to know more about him was acceptable but not preferable. She did not seem to be aware of her own behavior patterns and that it was herself about whom she needed to know more. She had completely bypassed any investigation of why she had been involved in so many disastrous affairs. At 37 years of age, there was also the question of what she had been doing with her life for the previous 18 years that made her feel she had not lived or existed until she met Dylan.

SEEKING IDENTITY THRU MALE PARTNERS

It appeared that she had been seeking her identity or persona through her male partners without being aware of her own worth or feeling good about herself as an individual. This would make it extraordinarily difficult for her to make any productive or insightful decisions at the onset of any relationship. She was also setting herself up for a powerful let-down should the object of her affections abdicate.

In therapy sessions that followed, she was helped to remember, accept and relive her feelings of low self esteem with reference to the source from which they had emanated. She came to understand how she had constantly sought the approval of others generally, and of men specifically, to build and maintain self acceptance. It gradually became clear to her how this had severely hampered her judgment when picking or allowing herself to be picked by potential suitors.

SEEKING REVENGE

In working with Dylan, who perceived himself as having been victimized financially and emotionally by two previous divorces, it was gradually made clear to him how he had unconsciously been seeking revenge—via several aborted liaisons. His love'em and leave'em attitude had yet to surface in his relationship with Laura. Judging from his past pattern of behavior, it was just a matter of time before she would be his next victim.

HIDDEN AGENDAS

After six months of being seen separately and together they were still hard at work on their individual problems and beginning to understand what it was like to become good friends. Except for Dylan's marriages, this was the longest relationship he had had since being divorced four years before. Their road to self realization was quite rocky but they are currently operating at a much more self enlightened level and with a healthier regard for each others feelings now that each of them has gotten in touch with the hidden agendas within themselves. The prognosis on this couple remains guarded, but each of them appears to have benefited greatly from what they have learned and feel much more secure about whatever decision either of them may make.

THE BUZZ WORD SELF-ESTEEM

One of the conflicts that rages in all our lives, it seems, is the basic need to be a separate and self functioning, competent adult, but if we are reasonably sane and human, we also have a need to be a part of another person's life by way of marriage or commitment, however briefly, to a meaningful other or make some kind of family or societal connection with another. We can resolve this conflict only when we are able to become vulnerable to another human being without feelings of loss of self esteem. The buzz word; it seems, in relationships is "self esteem". Without it, the individuals involved, especially in male-female relationships, are at a distinct disadvantage for several reasons. Choices based on low self esteem will almost always manifest how one feels about one's self, are emotional in context and will often run smack into the intellect which will not be able to tolerate the consequences of such a choice. Who we chose as a partner is a reflection of our judgment of character including our own. Those who hold themselves in high esteem are far less likely to put up with anyone treating them any worse than they would treat themselves.

People with low self esteem tend to attract, pick or be picked by others with low self esteem (the "others" with low self esteem are more clever at hiding it). So, our victims do not readily recognize it in "others" because in many cases they are not aware of it in themselves.

KNOWING WHEN TO TERMINATE THE RELATIONSHIP

We are, of course, all fallible and do not or cannot always detect, in advance or otherwise negative or unacceptable treatment from our partners. Those who are in touch with themselves and are self accepting (upon awareness of such treatment) will employ the best means possible to remedy the situation, keeping in mind the limitations they have set on their own tolerance levels, regardless of the emotional cost. When such levels are reached, self actualized individuals, after due consideration, will terminate the relationship temporarily or permanently, however reluctantly. They feel, and rightfully so, that loneliness is not an excuse for suffering bad company.

The recognition in each of us of our own flaws, the awareness and acceptance of both the light and dark sides of our persona and the ability to ultimately forgive (not forget) everything from small mistakes to horror stories wrought from and experienced during our childhood are all stepping stones that need to be walked upon or retraced in the therapeutic process toward self acceptance and self approval. Until we can tolerate and learn to live comfortably with what we know to be true of ourselves, we will find it very difficult to live with the flaws of others. Those who don't accept themselves as they really are, warts and all, will put an inordinate burden upon their mates to in some way compensate for this.

FROM "IN LOVE" TO TRUE LOVING

Ideally, the therapeutic process will bring about the realization that we all have flaws that can somehow sooner or later be forgiven or at least tolerated. Unsolved issues from childhood, however gross or negligible, idiosyncrasies, quirks, different perceptions and points of view will manifest themselves in your mate no matter how compatible your interests are. At the beginning of a relationship being "in love", often blinds us to the negative qualities of our mate. However intensely this "love" is experienced, sooner or later, the mate becomes a real person that makes real mistakes and doesn't always live up to your expectations. If you are not prone to see how you, too, fall into this category you will never be able to be graceful about it in your mate. It is at this point therapy or counseling can often help a couple out of the "in love" stage into actively loving and accepting each other stage which involves a lot more effort and focus.

Being "in love" is often a romantic notion usually based on strong physical or chemical attraction and sometimes is really only infatuation. The biggest delusion of being in this state is that there is an assumption that this circumstance will nurture and regenerate itself and will mature automatically. Not so. One of the best descriptions of the word love is the ability to want for your partner what that partner wants for him or her self—even if this means the partner wants time or space away from you. This feeling is the first step toward reducing budding power struggles between couples and the need to be in control.

UNCONDITIONAL LOVE

Another definition of love is the unconditional acceptance of one's partner. This is a much heralded and ideal premise and it is practically impossible when it concerns adults. A more reasonable premise would appear to be that you do not have to accept your mate's behavior or negative treatment of you unconditionally but you can still accept the person despite their behavior. Emotional negotiations are for your mate's behavior, not for his or her being. Unconditional love is, of course, much more complicated and difficult at the adult level. In the best of all possible worlds, we should all have experienced it during our childhood. Where emotional development was arrested by the lack of this experience, the result has been known to produce a frightened, insecure, needy, sometimes vindictive and, depending upon the degree of deprivation, even a psychopathic individual. Their self image is not only shaky and their real self is so submerged they are no longer in touch with the consequences of their own behavior or how it affects others. If they are still avidly seeking this total unconditional acceptance, and they don't have it to give or return, there is a tendency for them to feel frustrated or betrayed when it is not forth coming from their mate. Getting a fair share of unconditional love as children makes us a lot less needy as grownups and makes it easier to accept our partners on a more realistic basis. The communication created by this acceptance is the tool that keeps us from crossing over the line of no return with each other or punishing each other by way of verbal or physical aggression or withdrawal from the arena altogether.

MANY THERAPEUTIC APPROACHES

There are as many approaches to helping couples as there are couples. Some therapists find that using testing devices and or psychological evaluations (which often saves time and money for clients) are very productive as an introductory measure. How each partner responds to their feelings about the basics such as sex, money, life styles, hygiene, children and child rearing, in-laws, sharing of chores, etc. sets the stage for what needs to be addressed. The results of these tests often help the therapist pick up on the hidden agendas they discover. They can then not only help their clients see and acknowledge these tendencies but also gauge each partner's ability to cope with and resolve what they discover.

This type of analysis may seem to be a cold, calculating method of dealing with the unconscious levels of one's clients. But these revelations will surface sooner or later within the committed relationship often without any emotional preparation on the part of either partner to handle them.

Living a lie or hiding one's true persona in a committed relationship is possible but ultimately extremely difficult to sustain. Nobody likes nasty little surprises. Even if an unwelcome discovery that presents itself is not serious or intentional, the fact that it comes as a surprise is often enough to derail a relationship to the extent that it is difficult to get it back on track.

No matter how many tests are taken or how much analysis, therapy or counseling one goes through, there are always going to be instances of things going bump in the night that cannot be predicted, cured or solved. It's not possible to know everything about another person. People being human react differently under different circumstances at different times. What pre-marital therapy or counseling can do is prepare the participants for the unforeseen by way of better insight, productive disagreement or strategy before disastrous behavior occurs. When things go awry, as they are bound to, especially in the form of unwelcome surprises—the couple is at least armed with some skills with which they can negotiate a possibly amicable settlement of their disagreements.

CHAPTER 7

Reshaping Your Female Attitudes

There are relatively few adult or emotionally mature females (the two are not necessarily synonymous) who have not gained through their own life experience as well as through information fed to them by others, some expertise in the arena of the love game. For instance, they have found that it's not enough to just get a man, (most of us can get a man interested in us however temporarily,) the problem seems to be in securing some kind of sustained relationship with him. It's not that such women don't understand and desire such a relationship, but that they keep going to the wrong (for them) sources to achieve it.

BUILDING BARRIERS

Often, instead of using this or these negative experiences productively, they have a tendency to focus on the obstacles in their paths (which they, themselves, have often put there) which not only diverts them from their goal, but also predicts that it is unattainable. That state of affairs will almost certainly reinforce and solidify their not getting who or what they want. Some of the rather common obstacles are: "don't you know that there's a shortage of eligible men?" "It wouldn't matter if I had the beauty and talent of a Elizabeth Taylor or Lena Horne, there's not enough men to go around with whom I have something in common or who "measure up" (whatever that means). Statistically, it is true that (especially in the urban areas) there are more women then men. It would therefore eventuate that there are probably more "eligible" women than "eligible" men. Eligible is put in quotes here because it is too often confused with the word "available". More barriers: "Men are not always what they appear to be. They hide their feelings and/or they are secretive (the sin of omission) about their marital or "live-in" or girlfriend status. How can you trust them?"

CONSIDER BASKETBALL

Ladies, nobody promised you a rose garden. If you have ever played in or watched a basketball game you will note that a player's skill depends on sinking a shot with a guard waving his hands and arms in front of him obstructing him in every way possible. The guard is not going to step aside and give you carte blanche to the basket. That's not the reason, nor how the game is played. By focusing on the basket and not on the guard (except how to avoid him) the object of the player is not to retreat because of the opposition, but to slam-dunk in spite of it.

Has it occurred to you that men through experience (especially since females have become so liberated) have found that they do not have to be revelatory about their love or sex lives? This becomes increasingly more evident as they keep encountering women who are so inept, vulnerable, gullible or needy that they either miss or ignore the road signs that would give them some of the information they are seeking.

WHEN DOES TRUST BEGIN?

In chronological order, there shouldn't be a need to "trust" any man unless you have made some kind of decision or personal commitment known only to you, consciously or unconsciously (and the latter is more difficult to recognize) that you really wish to become involved in a relationship with him. Up to that point, his marital or otherwise involved status should be meaningless to you. We are proceeding on the assumption that you know what you want in a relationship and what your priorities are. Therefore, "trust" lies in your ability to trust yourself and your own judgment thereby rendering you willing to live with any choices you decide to make. It also means you have done some mental homework by way of keen observation of and attention to what is going on in your affair before reaching the point where you feel you've been "had".

SUPERWOMAN

So much for fooling around semantically. The facts may be that you are, or can be eminently attractive, reasonably well informed or educated, progressive, ambitious and to some degree, assertive. You can balance your own checkbook, pay your own rent (however reluctantly) and juggle a social and cultural life all the while holding down a job or business with the added possibility of being a single parent. In short, you sound and feel like a candidate for Superwoman.

CATCH 22

Now, if only you can find Superman who can equal, appreciate and share all of this. There's the catch 22. You'll be quick to note and thereby obstruct your own view by declaring that there are more of you than them. That state of affairs should enable you to immediately see that getting what you want has become a question of the survival of the fittest. Neither youth, beauty, intelligence or accomplishment necessarily warrant your winning the competition, if, indeed, that's how you view it. You know better than anyone else does that there are many women who fit all of the above and are still looking or waiting for Mr. Right. It can't be news to you that Cheek toothpaste, Miss Clarify or Acrid deodorant will nail down a permanent alliance with that one special male. Nor will performance via the latest kinky sexual technique keep him interested on a sustained basis, despite the avalanche of brainwashing by the media and porno peddlers. Everybody sees this and reads it (starting at an earlier age these days). You are not the only sexually liberated lady.

FOCUSING ON THE NEGATIVE

So what's the secret or secrets? I'm not so sure there are "secrets" out there as much as there are those parts of yourself that you are not aware of, may be hiding from or are really unconscious of, all of which (excluding dumb luck) you and only you can discover and control. For instance:

if you assume there are no men around who can measure up to your standards, then you will be seeking the standards. You will obliterate the man, himself, in which case almost every man will come up short. That, in turn, reinforces your original belief—that your not having a satisfactory lover or husband can be blamed on the lack of the criteria you have set up or are seeking. When this becomes the rule rather than the exception, you become conditioned to it and are inclined to focus (ultimately) on the negatives of the situation. When one focuses on the negative one sets up a pattern of getting the negative.

ALWAYS BEING RIGHT
Another instance of the enemy within (and we must consider it an enemy if it keeps us from getting what we want) is the perfectionist or the person who would rather be "right" (which is always subjective) or feel justified in their attitude, rather than get what they really want. The two are definitely not synonymous. Being right is a chilly thing to take to bed on a cold winter's night if you are seeking human warmth. If we could extend ourselves beyond our own belief systems of what's correct or "in", we could become more spontaneous or adventurous and might discover or help to create a whole Brave New World.

A third instance is a lack of open-mindedness, which means for some, it is a source of annoyance, resentment or outright rage when people don't fit into our pre-conceived, pre-programmed categories of behavior or life style. Many of us live in a world of "shoulds", "oughts" and "supposed-to-be's" rather than being able to accept the world of "is". There's a certain amount of profundity in the Black vernacular "it be's like that".

FEAR OF FAILURE
And last, but certainly not least, is that negative within us—the fear of failure—which is translated by some to mean not succeeding in reaching some desired goal. Nothing could be further from the truth. Because you do not "get" what you go after doesn't mean you are a failure. It only means that you simply didn't get what you went after (which may not have been good for you anyway). "Be careful what you want, you

may get it". Success versus failure has to be seen in terms of being a successful human being which means if you are a reasonably happy, comfortable and self-accepting (after all we do live in a very imperfect world), you are a success. As such you merely realize that the solution to not getting whatever you went after is to keep on trying, or if what you're after is that damned elusive or unattainable, knowing when to give it up and try for something else. (Children want what they can't have; grown-ups want what they can get and recognize the difference.)

LEGACY OF UPBRINGING

Most of us know, by now, that a lot of our behavior and feelings about ourselves have been passed on to us from our well-intentioned (and some not so well-intentioned) parents and significant others in our lives who may not have been aware of the subliminal negative vibes they were feeding us. Nevertheless, they were attitudes and feelings about ourselves and others that we absorbed at a time when we had no life experience, wisdom or outside support to challenge or combat. Some of us picked up the pattern of such thinking and donned it where our parents left off by continuing to view ourselves in the same way, thereby attracting similar negative reactions from our peers. But as adults, even if it's necessary to seek professional help, it is within our power to change such attitudes so we can go after what we want in relative freedom.

It seems the most important "secret" one can have about getting someone to love or care for you is that you can't "get" someone to do it. It is often a question of luck, the right chemistry, sometimes having much in common, other times having nothing in common. The formula seems to arise out of the historical, psychological needs of each partner. As close as you can come to activating such a situation is to know how to score brownie points for your own self while in no way taking or needing to take any away from your intended. Women who know what is important to themselves are those who know in advance what they want out of a relationship and do not (out of desperation—which we all experience) trade it off for whatever might (or in many cases might not) be offered to them. They also recognize that since we do not live in an altogether perfect world, none of us are ever going to get everything we want from it and that the next criteria boils down to how much we are willing to settle for.

WHAT TO SETTLE FOR
What you would be willing to settle for depends upon your value system. On a scale of one to ten, only you know if a "10" means he's a tall, dark handsome, successful brain surgeon. He may also be a cold, heartless bastard, Don Juan or insensitive clod, where you're concerned. On the other hand a "2" might be translated by you as a low-salaried, struggling apprentice who is not nearly as tall, dark and handsome but who happens to have potential, is warm, tender, faithful and cares about you. Sure, it would be nice to have a combination of the two but you would have to be willing to ignore the odds of such a "him" existing and being available. This is just another way of saying that the woman who is successful in finding her dreamboat realizes, considering the myriad of qualities possessed by everyone, that he's bound to achieve a nine in one area, a two in another, a seven in a third, etc. You could spend a lifetime with computers just figuring out the permutations of how he averages out.

That should make you more aware of the fact that it's not so much the kind of person he's portrayed as or what he possesses but rather how he feels about you, what he is offering you and how emotionally available he is to you.

WHAT HE SAYS VERSUS WHAT HE DOES
Are there any clues to let you know this aside from what you are being told by him which you might still be considering is just his "line"? The most prominent thing, which you need to view as objectively as possible, is what he does, how he perceives you and how he treats you. That's always much louder than what he says. For instance, a man will proclaim loudly and clearly that he is only interested in or prefers an intelligent and independent woman. He often honestly believes this especially as it pertains to a woman's ability to run a home, care for him and raise a family. However, at some point in time, he may perceive the fact that you are, indeed, quite smart and more than capable of

functioning independently on your own. For you, this does not mean you will love him less or are unwilling to share your capabilities with him, but for him it can and often does become threatening.

So it behooves you if you see this as becoming an emotional bargaining chip—to consider to what degree you can portray these qualities without bending him out of shape.

HOMELY AS A MULE
To deviate for a moment, we have all seen men who we thought were "fabulous," "cute" "a hunk" or whatever adjective most favorably expresses your vernacular for what seems like a great "catch." The woman he's with, however, often defies any explanation as to their relationship. She may well be a little brown wren or as homely as a mule. Nevertheless you have to admit they are an item which means she's probably got some quality invisible to you, but that certainly attracted him. It has been noted when talking with some of these women that they not only had, but also exuded (if you got close enough to experience it) a kind of quiet acceptance of and confidence in themselves and their femininity. They were generally very realistic about their status quo in the beauty market. Like the blind person who compensates for his or her blindness by developing a keen sense of awareness through other senses, they develop and cultivate, early on, those unseen but soothing qualities that beep like radar to the often generally harassed male. This does not mean that they are not professional, bright, competent and assertive when the occasion calls for it, but they evinced a strong sense of what they not only wanted but also expected to get. This kind of realistic appraisal and acceptance of themselves spills over into their appraisal and acceptance of others. They were aware (via society) of their limitations (which we all have) without being hampered by them. In short, their focus was not on society's negative appraisal, but unwaveringly on what they wanted for themselves.

BELIEVE IN YOURSELF
Once you learn to ignore the obstacles (which means you have consciously or otherwise accepted the fact that they exist), that should leave you a lot

of energy to concentrate on ways of bypassing or getting around them. The first thing you need is to have a genuine belief that you deserve and are therefore always in the process of getting who and what you want, no matter what your previous track record has been. The unconscious has no past or future...only the now which is an accumulation of your psychological history up to this very moment. It acts upon what it is fed daily and momentarily and if you are still giving it orders from the past or attempting to program it for the future, while ignoring its nowness, it has a tendency to remain stagnant or to regress to a former status quo.

The second ability you need is to "flow" as a fighter does, as he moves around the ring. Even when he gets hit (and he does, often) he continues to move, bob and weave to get the advantage over his opponent. It's difficult to hit a moving target, so the more you keep your feelings flowing, the more places they will have to go and explore. You will not be so radically handicapped by a setback even when your interest and efforts are ignored. Women, it seems, fear alienation from meaningful others much more than men. Early on, they learn how to tolerate, cooperate, and negotiate in order to avoid feelings of being rejected or abandoned. Unfortunately, this often leads them into entering relationships too quickly, too intensely or without checking the detour signs along the way or reading the handwriting on the wall. Often, in short order, they leap frog from the first few dates to fantasizing about a new last name or walking down a church aisle with an unsuspecting, potential groom.

They are so goal focused on their destination they don't get to enjoy the trip.

THE INTERVIEW PROCESS
Reshape your thinking. If you have on occasion found yourself in this thinking mode, it is something you should definitely re-consider. The dating process should be one of friendly interview and observation while understanding that simultaneously you are also learning about how you are reacting to this person you are discovering. This will help you to become cognizant of what it is about him that attracts you and if that attraction is substantial enough for you to continue the dating

game with him. If you are not overwhelmed by your feelings for him (and you certainly need to be aware of this if you are) you need to really listen to him talk about himself. This is the interview process whereby you can begin to ascertain his character, value system and goals early on in the relationship. This is also the time to find out about his opinions and beliefs about what is important to you. Hopefully, you should already be on very familiar terms with how you personally feel about these same issues yourself. For example; what are his religious beliefs, does he prefer urban to suburban or country living, does his energy level match yours, how does he feel about abortion, the death penalty, civil rights, politics, racism, child rearing, money issues? Is he athletic, active or a couch potato, does he have close friends, does his personal hygiene meet with your approval etc?

Equally as important is some knowledge of his personality such as how he handles anger or adversity when things don't go his way. Does he have the ability to trust, to maintain protracted or lasting friendships? Does he appear to be well received or liked by the meaningful others in his life? How does he handle himself or interact with strangers, waiters, bosses? Does he consider any people his inferiors or superiors and if so how does he relate to them? You can pick up more clues to his personality by knowing what kind of relationship he had or has with his parents—particularly how he feels about his father (if one was in evidence) and his past and current relationship with his mother.

These are not issues on which you question or confront him. Rather, if you know how to pace yourself, it is knowledge you will gradually gain about him over a period of time while being in his company.

BEING A GOOD LISTENER

The best communication is in knowing how to be a good listener. There are ways without being intrusive or employing the methods of the paparazzi that can get your friend to open up to you—particularly about his past from at least high school days as well as what he sees as his future. He may tend to bottle up on the present because he does not necessarily want to be held accountable in case things don't go according to his plans. Listening in a mode of general acceptance without making verbal value judgments go a long way toward loosening him up. Directing his conversation toward your own areas of interest (where applicable) or introducing these subjects as something you heard or read via the media, will reduce suspicion that he is being interviewed. Using body language to convey total interest in the subject under discussion often encourages men to reveal more of themselves. This is not the time to evaluate, criticize or reject out of hand whatever the opinion or subject matter happens to be. You will only succeed in having him argue his point more vociferously, drop the subject altogether or change his presentation, ideas or facts to please you or mold them to what he believes is more to your liking or acceptance. If this happens you will not get a true picture of his personality and you may be setting yourself up for some unpleasant discoveries at a later date.

FIND OUT WHAT HE IS LOOKING FOR
Part of your interview process should include ascertaining what he wants in a woman, mentally, physically and emotionally. Its better to find out early in the relationship how close you come to his ideal. This is especially true of those males who feel they can settle for nothing less. If you are light years away from or in some cases even a short distance from what he requires, especially physically and you find out he has broken up with other women who didn't meet his standards, expect that his displeasure with you will ultimately surface. It's only a matter of time before he will be off searching for those missing qualities in someone else. Need some clues as to how he is disposed towards you? It's a wake-up call if he subtly plagues you or harps on something he considers a physical flaw or life style shortcoming with regard to your weight, your hair style, your make up, the size of your body parts, your personal environment, your mental outlook, etc. Be prepared to make changes in these areas if that is your solution to maintaining the relationship or accept the fact that if you don't, you won't be accepted as you are and assume that this is his way of grooming you for his exit.

OLD BUT WISE ADVICE

The following is advice you must have heard from at least three generations of mothers. Don't be in a hurry to share sexual relations with your new friend. When you do, you need to be the one to set the pace, passively or actively, for the time, place and frequency. The dating and friendship part of a relationship between men and women seems to change significantly for women when sex enters the picture. All sorts of expectations tend to accompany the feelings that are aroused by sexual intimacy in women—especially if she considers that sex is special and the sex with him is spectacular. This seems to be more the rule than the exception. In men it's almost the opposite. This does not mean that men don't or can't feel or want to feel closer and more loving after having slept with a woman but it's a crap shoot depending upon what unconscious feelings were triggered in the man. In some cases he may feel trapped or guilty because of his lack of feeling for her or it may give him a sense of proprietorship in that now this woman belongs to him. In others, it merely makes him boastful or exalted about his prowess and in some cases he may, even find he has genuine feelings of love for the woman. Even so, none of these feelings will prohibit him from possibly becoming sexually involved or remaining involved in the future with other sleep mates.

THE CHANGING ROLE OF MEN

When statistics tell us that 70% of women are in the work place, married or single, and that between 50% and 60% of homes are single parented (98% by the mother only) it can be concluded that women may want but do not need men in their previous capacity either as breadwinners or authoritarian patriarchs in the household. In speaking with most working lower middle to upper middle class women, the consensus of opinion is that they want and need men for intimacy, bonding, communication and for the sharing of feelings and life styles. In the interviewing process (assuming this is what you too are seeking) it can be difficult to discover if your partner has the potential for this kind of relationship. Nevertheless, every effort needs to be put forth to ascertain if your chosen one does indeed have the capacity for this kind of togetherness.

TRUE INTIMACY

Having a healthy ego and healthy self esteem (see chapter II) are the cornerstones and necessary elements of true intimacy (not sexual intimacy). This is intimacy which involves the ability to give and receive, be vulnerable and loyal, have respect, tolerance and patience for your mate and be able to handle betrayal. Although this kind of intimacy comes easier to women that men, there are women who have difficulty with it also especially when it involves openness and trust. They often don't trust their own cut-off point should the affair begin to deteriorate, which would benefit their own best interests. So they are therefore reluctant to demonstrate acceptance and understanding of their partner's unique needs and goals. It's fodder for comedians that women will withhold intimacy, sexual and non-sexual, when displeased with a partner's deeds, performance or life style. In many cases, like men, this retaliation can apply to some immutable characteristics of their partners, such as age, cultural background, ethnicity, height, or physical handicap none of which can necessarily be changed. Other negative but legitimate attitudes harbored by women can be the result of childhood trauma such as verbal, physical or sexual abuse, rejection, abandonment and or neglect. A history of any of these incidents can create anything from a clinging possessive personality to an inordinate need and craving for revenge or attention which is often obtained by what others might interpret as bizarre or unacceptable behavior.

SELF EVALUATION

Some clues that you need to be aware of and employ in your relationship with yourself and others is recognizing when:

1. You are doing more and more for less and less—rather than doing more only when it gets you your desired results.
2. You see yourself as only coping and surviving rather than living and thriving.

3. You have little or no desire or focus for self-directed activity or goals, rather than have interesting self absorbing hobbies or projects.

4. You are continuously attempting to bond with a narcissistic personality rather than learn why you can't relate to a partner with whom you share similar feelings and interest.

5. You behave as a result of compliance or easily make compromises rather than act out of negotiation and mutual agreement.

6. You go along with a program to keep peace, although inwardly being against it rather than do that with which you are comfortable and choose to do.

7. You make exceptions for bad behavior in your mate which you would not accept in any one else rather than share a standard of behavior which although can be flexible remains the basis of your beliefs.

8. You react by quickly altering your own circumstances or status quo to fit the molds and plans of others rather than act by understanding others situation while remaining focused on your own mood and plans.

9. You generally feel you are trapped in circumstances beyond your control rather than be aware that you always have choices and need to feel free to act upon them.

10. You are so strongly influenced by your feelings for your mate that they become an obsession rather than understand the gravitational pull and see it as only information about yourself.

In the end, are you "in love" with him or do you "love" him and want for him what he wants for himself? Do you want or need him as a trophy, a breadwinner, a possession, a prize, someone to take away the loneliness (keep in mind one should not trade loneliness for bad company), an escort, a provider, or someone upon whom you can ultimately take out all your anger and frustrations against males in general to make up for father hunger or other deprivations? If any of these reasons for your relationship strike a chord, you are not ready for the kind of adult relationship that has the best chance of making it over the long haul.

CHAPTER 8

Reshaping Your Male Attitudes

This chapter is not about male bashing. It will instead, hopefully help men to not only understand themselves and their mates better but also recognize that there are certain male characteristics of behavior that appear to be universal. As such, these characteristics will only be changed by those men who see a need to change as a form of enlightened self interest.

THE EYES HAVE IT
Men are definitely more attracted to women by what they see, at least at the initial meeting. And if they are very attracted at this instance this often carries over into a kind of infatuation. At this juncture, it is not unusual for the female if she is similarly attracted to believe that she is the chosen one. This is a situation from which it makes it very difficult for the male to then extricate himself. This is especially true if along the line, he realizes she does not have the inner qualities or other character traits he desires.

So, part of the dating game for men is not only also interviewing her but also listening and carefully observing the signals and clues she gives about her inner self. This not only does well for continuing the courtship should this be a mutually desirable goal, it also staves off the urgency of you bedding your companion prematurely. In short, you need to understand the importance of becoming friends with a woman before allowing lust or passion to overwhelm you unless that's all that interests the both of you.

REVIEW RELATIONSHIP WITH PARENTS

Before becoming involved at a deeper level, assuming that you are interested in furthering the union, it would be helpful for you to review and understand your relationship with your mother, your feelings for your father (assuming one was in evidence) or his absence which will also evoke certain feelings and behaviors. If you grew up with two parents, the dynamics you observed between them goes a long way toward telling you what you expect in a marriage and how you will behave in one. Generally women have a need for closeness and intimacy (again not sexual) but for many men (who have the same needs) it's difficult for them to acknowledge this need because it involves vulnerability. When you can acknowledge your deepest feelings involving your fears, griefs and or past errors, it's a step in the direction of accepting your own humanity and it is an ability that is inordinately appealing to women.

WHAT WOMEN NEED

Being able to supply comfort and touch that is non-sexual in nature, being a good listener, and having the ability to emphasize or at least sympathize with your mate are admirable and welcome traits. Being non-competitive in the inner sanctum of your relationship, relinquishing the reins of being head honcho when an existing situation would be better served by your doing so, all go a long way to creating the kind of harmony so avidly sought by couples.

Because men and maybe you, are generally solution oriented, they are often quick to criticize, give an opinion or advise on how to clear up a problem when sometimes their mate only wants an attentive, non-judgmental ear or someone to just listen. This male characteristic is quickly defined by women as you not wanting to hear the problem or story and therefore you offer quick fix-it solutions to end the complaint. This is often the basis of some of the built up resentment women feel against men.

BRIDGING TWO WORLDS

We live in a society today where the roles of men and women are so blurred and the rules of partnerships have changed and continue to change so drastically it becomes increasingly difficult to implement them. It's no longer commonplace for "the little woman" to stay at home and be totally and only occupied with the raising of children and household chores while the man gets to be out in the workaday world and "brings home the bacon." Togetherness is a much more multifaceted endeavor which means husbands are expected to share their daily experiences with their wives, while also maintaining (as do women) separate interests. So a good part of your commitment to each other is your willingness to not only include your mate in your daily life, but to also have fun together, learn how to tolerate each other's flaws, find interests common to both of you and to share your opinions and feelings about what is going on in both of your worlds.

VALUE OF HUMOR

There are some qualities that really need to be cultivated in order to sustain a working relationship with your mate. Initial meetings do not reveal a man's character, nor do the first few dates. A woman needs to be in the company of a man for a protracted period of time to learn whether or not he is sane, humane, kind, honest, dependable, loyal, well mannered, hygienically acceptable, etc. (assuming these are qualities she desires in a mate.) It's equally important that you be able to offer genuine friendship which is the basis for sharing interests. It's a plus if you have a sense of humor which includes your ability to be amused at yourself and the absurd as well as have the ability to maintain your balance in the midst of chaos. Too often, in uncomfortable situations men translate their feelings into unexplainable action, passive aggressive behavior or silence which over a period of time, is bound to erode a partnership. If you can communicate your feelings about your emotions both negative and positive rather than playing the strong silent type, clamming up or acting out in a way that often leaves a woman either confused or feeling guilty this will go a long way towards helping your relationship to survive.

VULNERABILITY

Intimacy should not be a key word for sex but it often is to men. Its more profound meaning is sometimes threatening or frightening to a man because it means sharing his self doubts, emotional needs, and weaknesses as well as his hopes and dreams of the future with his loved one. If you, who are reading this, need to be macho and always manifest the image of being able to take care of yourself without any emotional help, support or dependence upon anyone else, you will be unable to be there for your mate to fulfill her emotional needs because of your inability to acknowledge or recognize them in yourself.

All of the above assumes that these are qualities most women want and need in a mate, however, there truly are different strokes for different folks. The possession of a lot of these characteristics depends upon whether or not your paramour requires them and could be happy with you who may not possess all these sterling qualities. So be it, but that too is determined by compatibility which is not so much doing or being the right thing or person respectively, but being and doing what mutually satisfies both you and your mate.

CHECKLIST

Some reflections and personal observations that are food for thought for you as well as your mate:

1. Solid relationships appear to have as a hall mark sustenance with the continual disappearance of illusions.
2. You came into this world alone—even if you were a twin—and will leave alone. You need to learn how to be comfortably alone with yourself without being self destructive.
3. It's normal to be sometimes jealous, demanding, impatient, disinterested, controlling or self absorbed so long as at least an equal or more amount of your time is spend in your being forgiving, interested, patient, concerned, tolerant thoughtful, understanding and supportive. The former should be the exception, rather than the rule.
4. It takes restraint to learn this but offering criticism or immediate solutions is less acceptable than sometimes just listening.

5. Going into a relationship with a person with unactualized potential, or with the intent of changing that person into your ideal is folly.
6. Concentrating on changing or correcting your own flaws or those which are perceived as such by your mate is more important than concentrating on or pointing out his or hers.
7. A lot of your reactions to your female mate is based upon the effect of the relationship between you and your parents, especially your mother.
8. When you find yourself irresistibly drawn to the attractiveness and charisma of another that's more a sign of what your basic needs are rather than the charm of the object of your affections. Charm, like beauty, is in the eye of the beholder.
9. Pay attention to what you find negative or unacceptable in others. It probably reflects some unacknowledged part of yourself.
10. Forgiveness and enlightened self interest is the food of love, no matter how long either of them takes to render or experience.
11. If it doesn't automatically happen for us emotionally, we need to find ways intellectually to learn how to love and accept ourselves. Without this ability we cannot truly love and accept another.
12. Love is an active verb, not a state into which one finds one has fallen.
13. Closing the door on pain, frustration, anger, hate, grief, resentment, sorrow and regret is also shutting out joy, acceptance, love, interest, caring, consideration, enthusiasm, and ecstasy.
14. Loving another, regardless of whether or not it is reciprocated takes nothing from us. It only enriches us with the knowledge that we can love.
15. When your own boundaries and needs are intact and clear to you respectively, only then can you relate to a partner with whom mutual love can exist.
16. You are on the road to emotional maturity when most of your behavior is governed by agreement, acceptance or negotiation, compromise and flexibility.

17 No matter what you say or profess, your conduct comes across much louder. Others will trust you in accordance with how they perceive your behavior.

18 The more alive we really are the greater our capacity to both give and receive.

CHAPTER 9

She Says, He Hears, He Says, She Hears

It appears to be firmly established that there is a tremendous communication gap between men and women and that it is necessary for both sexes to understand each other better, by understanding why. Since women are more familiar with the emotional need for compromise and negotiation for intimacy (despite the risk of suffering emotional pain) they appear to need to be in the forefront of having to understand men as well as their lack of communication skills.

Some of the reasons men and women are so different in the way they communicate verbally:

1. THEIR SOCIALIZATION PROCESS is quite different from females. They are taught early on how to "do" rather than feel, quickly solve problems, achieve status in the competitive world of men, etc., in order to avoid being labeled a failure. They are not focused in on "grey" emotional areas since to them, their goals are power, status and accomplishment. This state of affairs is perpetuated by men's reading material in their magazines and other media messages which are more likely to deal with sports, politics, entertainment and the external female form. Articles on relationships, emotional negotiation, the handling of feelings and caring about needs of members of the opposite sex are practically non-existent in male oriented magazines. Such articles, however, are the very breath of life in women's magazines.

2. WOMEN'S COMMUNICATIONS are designed to ward off alienation, by negotiation for closeness, the nurturing of compromise, friendship and intimacy. This does not mean that women are not currently interested in status and accomplishment, but like men, their priority is established on a different goal.

3. DURING THE MATURATION PROCESS in most ethnic groups, the small male child (especially one who may have grown up in a single mother household which is often true of Blacks who may not have had a male role model—experiences this larger than life female authority figure (for at least the first 15 to 16 years of his life) as unassailable. However benign or cruelly discipline, guidance or attention was administered by this female it will have a lot to with his response to peer group females as an adult.

EXAMPLE: if this young male had a domineering intrusive mother who exhibited a great deal of negative attitude and behavior toward her son, as an adult, when a wife or partner notes he is depressed or non-communicative and asks to share in or find out what his problem is, their respective intentions are often at odds.

HER AGENDA: "Something is wrong, my partner is shutting me out or he seems to have some kind of problem that is taking away our closeness. I want to help if I can so we can share whatever it is thereby maintaining and strengthening our relationship."

HIS AGENDA: Can be any of the following: "answering, getting into or extending this conversation will only make me feel worse." "This is an intrusion of my privacy. I'm a man, I should be able to solve my own problem." "She's pushing into my affairs, trying to control me, smothering me." "If I divulge my problem, I associate the consequences with the fact that I could be ridiculed, laughed at, upbraided, given faulty advice, thought less of." Any of these reactions depends upon his early experience with meaningful female authority figures.

EXAMPLE: She's had a recent negative experience at the office that has upset her emotionally and needs to complain about it to her mate.

HIS AGENDA: She's making a big fuss over something that's a no-brainer. I don't need to know all these details. She needs to get to the point. She should just tell the guy off or quit the damn job. She doesn't see what mistakes she made. There's nothing I can do about this.

HER AGENDA: I need to go into detail or a blow by blow description so he will not only understand what I'm feeling but why. I feel better being able to talk about it. I could use a verbal hug, or some sympathy and understanding for my point of view. Maybe I'll come up with a solution while I'm discussing it but right now I just want some one to commiserate with me, not criticize me, tell me what I did wrong or even how to fix it. If I want advice I'd like him to wait till I ask for it.

Men often wonder why the bond between women and their female friends is so strong and unassailable. It's one of the few contexts in which women can experience the relief the feeling of sympathy brings in times of stress, chaos, joy or during what they consider the more important events of their lives.

4. GIRLS AND BOYS START OUT dealing with conflict differently. Girls will at first attempt to talk out a problem in a conciliatory fashion with an eye to negotiating a compromise in order to avoid being isolated. Boys will use threats or often resort to physical violence as part of their "do" personality.

5. MEN SEE MAKING CONFESSIONS or talking about their deepest feelings as a sign of weakness or wimpishness, exposing them to being low man in the one-up-manship game. Women are more willing to risk telling it all in the hopes of the payoff of establishing further intimacy. Unfortunately it does not always work out this way putting the female in a position to be later victimized by her revelations.

6. IN THE CASE OF BLACK MEN AND WOMEN, the problem of communication is compounded, often because statistically, there is no male role model whereby male youngsters can experience the dynamic that occurs between male and female parents. Black males often find themselves in a hostile world where the social, political and economic odds are stacked against them by a white majority with which they have had to almost totally identify without ever having the sanction, permission or support to imitate. At the same time, they must also deal with being the cause of pain and frustration in their female counterparts who often view them as coming up short. Is it any wonder that men fear truly open communication with women, where indulging in intimacy might result in female disapproval or their possible dependency on women?

7. ALL THEIR LIVES MEN, Black or otherwise, have been taught in their competitive workaday business world (in which they spend at least one-third of their life where it pays to play it close to the vest) to remain closed and aggressive and reveal as little as possible to their business rivals. It hardly seems fair to expect them to come home, do a 180 degree turn and be spontaneously open to their mate about their deepest misgivings, problems and/or feelings.

8. ALSO, AS UNFAIR AS IT SEEMS, because most women have built in role models and are better at being in touch with their emotions, they are again elected to lead the way for men to open up and share themselves as well as support them in liberating themselves from their old stereotypes as women have done.

9. BOTH MEN AND WOMEN'S APPROACH to communication is valid, but men need to realize that women have already entered their world and are putting forth a great deal of effort to communicate positively with them. Men can only positively co-exist with women by being willing to learn how to negotiate living in a woman's world (without fear of giving up their masculinity) by sharing household chores, child rearing, coping with the extended family network in problem solving, etc. This should be done before either party commits to what may potentially become a disastrous relationship or marriage.

10. A GREAT MANY PROBLEMS IN a relationship surface as a result of one or in some cases both partners suffering from depression. It is important to be able to recognize the clues of depression because men and women handle and manifest them so differently. In the case of men, their behavior does not always include the signposts or signals of depression found in women. Men often manifest feelings of depression by aggressive, pugilistic or visibly self destructive behavior involving alcoholism, drug abuse, workaholism, womanizing, criminal activity, etc. They tend to project their negative feelings of self outwardly. Their behavior is not often indicative of what one would expect from a person who is experiencing depression.

Women, on the other hand, tend to send clearer signals of depression, manifested through visible sadness, inactivity, self neglect, social withdrawal, and/or general disinterest in the world around them. They too, often indulge in self destructive behavior such as overeating, over sleeping, inordinate indulgence in alcohol or drugs. However, they are more readily and easily recognized as depressives because they are more prone to discuss their feelings. Because of their need to air and share these feelings they more readily come to the attention of the statisticians, thereby upping the percentages of women appearing to suffer more from depression than men.

One solution to opening up communications between men and women is not to wait until impasses or stalemates are encountered in an already committed situation—such as marriage—but start learning each others language by way of pre-marital or just couples counseling (for those who do not wish to marry but still want to maintain a relationship). Counseling is still strongly recommended so that consciousness raising of each of the partner's emotional baggage can be brought out into the open under secure circumstances so that the couple can more clearly understand the he/speak, she/speak confrontations that are bound to occur in their ongoing relationship.

CHAPTER 10

It Is The Small Stuff That Counts

No matter how many observations, rules or strategies we employ in a relationship there are no fail safe formulas that will cover every contingency. Each person's conditioning and experience during their maturation years is as unique as a fingerprint. Sometimes, even after a couple has lived together for 5 or more years, they will still get divorced shortly after they marry. The clues to this turn of events often lie in the minutiae of life. It is more likely than not the little annoying things that send one or both members of a relationship over the edge, an edge of which neither of them were aware until they got to it. Complaints, some of which are more serious than others, made by warring couples are small things such as men not putting the toilet seat down, not asking for directions when lost, not putting the cap back on the toothpaste, one leaving dishes, trash or dirt to be cleaned or cleared out by the other, making unacceptable noises, singing off key, being talkative or disgustingly cheerful early in the morning, interrupting or finishing a mate's story, always needing to be the center of attention or life of the party, not listening when being spoken to, airing personal problems in public, constantly preening in the mirror, chewing with one's mouth open, daily hiding behind a newspaper, one constantly questioning the other about their whereabouts, being quick to scold, berate or criticize and would you believe, sleeping with one's socks on!

A SYMPTOM OF WHAT IS REALLY WRONG

Of course, any couple that decides to separate and divorce because of any one of these or an equally minor reason is really dealing with a symptom or manifestation of whatever is really wrong. Often the real problem has not so much to do with the perpetrators as how the recipient of their behavior reacts to it. Assuming that both people in a relationship are comfortable with their basic values, communication and views on social issues, sexual compatibility, finances, religion, child rearing, etc. the next step to explore in the context of their compatibility is their tolerance level of each other's peccadilloes and idiosyncrasies. There needs to be an acknowledgment of each partner's feelings about the other's quirky and or sometimes repellent behavior. Without this kind of airing, it is too easy to use your partner's behavior to mask a deeper conflict that can send you on the road to separation and divorce.

EXPECTATION AND DISAPPOINTMENT

If I were take a vote on the most overwhelming reason for wanting to exit from a relationship I would pick disappointment. The greater the disappointment, the greater the expectations were of the disaffected party. A good rule of thumb is that the only person of whom one should have great expectations is oneself. No matter how great the fanfare is for or about someone else, the same way that person can be the greatest thing since sliced bread, they can also not be. There is no up without a down. The complete picture is that at any given time, the behavior of another and your reaction to it can go in any direction. Emotionally mature people know this and learn early on in relationships to ride with the tide and roll with the punches. You can't do either of these until you first acknowledge that the tide and the punches exist.

There are behaviors in your mate that you will view as unacceptable and negative feelings you will experience as a result and over which sometimes you will have no control. Knowing this about yourself in advance gives you the opportunity to separate the wheat from the chaff—that is, quickly surmise which behaviors are really worth your getting your intestines into an uproar over. When presented with an unpleasant scenario, is it one you can survive, ignore, accept or resign yourself to without getting too bent out of shape? Will you be able to correctly assume that sometimes, despite your objections, the scenario will eventuate any way but doesn't really put your relationship at risk? Do you believe you have the wisdom to know how to weigh the behavior that annoys you against an otherwise good relationship and come up with a fair conclusion? Both the unacceptable behavior that elicits a reaction and the reaction are dynamics that each person should know. The big issues are much more evident and usually by mutual consent are either negotiable or not. The small ones don't necessarily have to be negotiated and in many instances can be overlooked, paid less attention to or turned into a source of amusement.

DEALING WITH CONFLICT

If your mate has basic humane qualities, a value system and life style compatible with yours, is your friend, is someone you trust, realize that there will still be bad times as well as good ones. Just because on occasion you disagree or find your mate's conduct not to your liking doesn't mean that your marriage is failing. In a good relationship couples learn quickly how to deal with conflict, directly or indirectly. They understand how important timing is. It's not necessarily a good idea to broach a prickly subject before dinner, or just after a person has crossed the threshold coming home from a hard day's work or just before retiring for the night. Resorting to passive-aggressive behavior such as sulking, stone walling silence, or vehemently denying the problem, may make you feel better but it will not make brownie points with your mate. The lines of communication need to stay open whether they're being used or not. Neither of you can expect the other to be a mind reader. You both need to be able to tell, ask for, say (not demand) what you are thinking and feeling without fear of reprisal, censure, withdrawal by the other, destructive criticism or abandonment. However, part and parcel of this caveat is learning and knowing enough about your partner to understand what borderlines should not be crossed or recognizing the point of no return before you reach it. There are instances where a painful verbal assault or statement can either close the door completely on further communication or send the relationship into such a tailspin, it would take a Herculean effort to pull it out before it crashes and burns.

"IN LOVE" INSTEAD OF LOVING

Anyone who has ever been "in love" knows how good it feels, as long as the euphoria lasts, and what a sense of well being one experiences. Note the term "in love." Actually, loving another, which may not be accompanied by being loved in return, is a whole other ball game. So let's distinguish between the two. Being "in love" means both parties are bathing in the approbation of each other and suggests a passive acceptance of a very ecstatic status quo. Really loving some one actively promises no recognition or reciprocation and can be done close up or at a distance without hope of reward. However, if one is going to spend the emotional energy to love another and hopefully be loved in return, there's a few other ingredients involved in the recipe if one is interested in sustaining a long term relationship:

1) TRULY LIKING the object of your affections. This is number one of at least four more ingredients needed to sustain a committed relationship, not necessarily in this order.

2) FRIENDSHIP which involves trust and an almost unconditional acceptance of the other's personality traits, however trivial or bizarre.

3) EMOTIONAL SUPPORT which involves the understanding of each others needs and goals and "being there" for your partner

4) AN ABILITY TO MAKE A COMMITMENT of exclusivity to your mate, in that no matter what other platonic or other liaisons you may have they will not have the privacy and intimacy you share with your spouse.

5) A SHARING OF SOME COMMON INTERESTS, value system, life style, ethics and morals. This does not mean you have to be twins joined at the hip. Two people can have two completely different personalities and originate from two different cultures, and still share all of the above ingredients in couplehood or marriage. What is important here is that these inner qualities are found in people of all national, geographical, ethnic or religious background. I often conduct couplehood counseling for couples coming from diverse backgrounds where some cultural differences could pose some unsurmountable conflicts.

CASE HISTORY

One such couple, a young, smart, chic Black woman, Naomi from Barbados W.I. and David an Asian from Hong Kong came in for two months of pre-marital counseling. They had been seeing each other for almost three years. They had met at a university from which they had both received degrees in the fine arts. Because of their love for art, they had opened and were running their own art and sculpture garden in the suburbs. Their families were friendly with each other and were very accepting of the relationship.; Their reason for coming into therapy was to discuss dealing with reactions they had experienced and that they were bound to continue to experience by people who did not approve of interethnic marriages. They were also concerned about how the fall out, if any, might affect their children. At the beginning they scored very similarly on the compatibility and E.Q. (Emotional Quotient) tests. During the course of two months they came to learn how strong the bond was between them and how deeply they shared ingredients they felt they needed to sustain their relationship despite any projected opposition to their union. Last year, they were recently wed in a ceremony of both cultures and so far are quite happy.

CASE HISTORY

Another couple, Christina, a Caucasian of Irish and French descent and Teddy who was half Native American and half Afro-American had met in high school in a small town in the south and found it difficult to pursue their relationship there. Christina moved to New York was in her third year at Columbia Teachers College when she ran into Teddy at a Christmas party. He had also moved to New York a year before, after graduating from a small southern college, to take a job with a publishing firm. It appears they picked up their friendship where it had left off and a year later came in for premarital counseling. It was clear aside from the other tests, that these two had a great deal in common, and were genuinely supportive of each other. Neither one, it seemed wanted to imagine life without the other and their feelings for each other had withstood a period of more than five years of not even seeing each other. After three months of counseling they were finishing each other sentences. The keystone to their relationship appeared to be their ability and desire to be genuinely interested in what each other wanted or was doing and a willingness to help each other achieve it. They were very aware of each others idiosyncrasies and annoying habits and seemed to be able to view them with more amusement than irritation. They married two years ago, despite the misgivings of one of the sets of in-laws (who none the less, attended the wedding) in an extra ordinarily beautiful ceremony and they are now the proud parents of twin boys. At last report they related they were happily sharing house work and baby care.

CASE HISTORY
A third couple Rhonda and Edward both Caucasians grew up in the same suburban neighborhood in Connecticut, graduated from the same college at the same time and shared the same religious background. They did not become serious about each other until they had been out of college for five or six years and had already launched into their respective careers, she, a lawyer and he an account executive. It was clear that by the time they decided to come in for pre-marital counseling the bloom was off the rose. They had decided to move in together shortly after some well heated sexual encounters and were into their eighth month of what appeared to be a rocky road relationship. Despite what each of them acknowledged was a pretty torrid sex life, their eight months of living together exposed some high profile conflicts in their personalities, social consciousness, character, value system, levels of emotional maturity as well as personal habits that made it very difficult for them to coexist peacefully. For example, he was for the death penalty, she was against it, he was a neat freak and somewhat of a perfectionist while she was much more casual and less particular about her surroundings. He

would often refer to her as a bleeding heart liberal while she considered him a reactionary. She was looking forward to having children while he remained very luke warm to the idea. She loved music (which she played all day long) and dancing and liked to have the house adorned with flowers and aromas all of which appeared to be lost on him and to which he was either totally oblivious or in which he was totally disinterested. He was somewhat of a loner, did not necessarily care to spend a lot of time with friends or relatives or going out and socializing while she, on the other hand spend a great deal of time talking with her pals on the phone and often arranged social events which he would occasionally refuse to attend. Their biggest blind spot was that each of them wanted the other to change rather than each of them accepting their mate as they were. There were both large and small differences which they could not surmount and upon which they could barely compromise. Their sex life was not enough glue to really hold them together. At their last visit, they agreed to living in separate quarters and giving each other some space. They also decided to continue therapy separately to become more familiar with themselves in the hopes of arriving at a more informed decision if and when they decided to pick up their relationship at a later date.

SIMILAR BACKGROUNDS

To a greater degree, sameness in economic, class, religious and life style background appears to breed stability and comfort. However, differences in other areas, such as physically or in personality can generate energy, controversy and spice up one's sex life especially if they are complimentary and can therefore make life much more interesting. The trick is to find a balance between the two that is comfortable for both parties.

CHAPTER 11

The Potential Extension of Marriage – Children

The psychological and emotional health of your child or children has, as its source, not only the nature of your relationship to each other but also both of your attitudes feelings and decisions about even having children. It is the singular most important decision in your marriage upon which you both need to definitely agree. If you are equally in favor of parenting it will contribute largely toward the well being of your potential offspring. There are no guarantees, however, and no matter how happy a couple is about becoming parents, things can still go wrong often without the parents' awareness or intent which can cause aberrant behavior in their children. Even slight negative nuances of attitudes and behavior between parents can be picked up by children. If parents are aware of this and how negatively perceived certain images may be impacting upon their child, they can investigate, discuss or explain to their children the reality of a given situation. Otherwise, children with their limited life experiences and emotional immaturity make up their own scenarios, which, if not clarified by a watchful parent can and often does exercise a traumatic influence on the child's life and future behavior. Suffice it to say that an ounce of prevention here is really worth a pound of cure. The more in cinque partners are with each other and the more they agree on having children and child rearing practices, the better off their youngsters will be.

24/7 COMMITMENT

This is a delicate area of your relationship that needs to be carefully explored before making a commitment to marriage. No matter how much two people love each other chances are that the entrance into their lives of a third party (or more) will occupy 90% of their time twenty-four-seven for at least the first four or five years of the child's life. Not only will this alter your life style considerably—it is bound to some degree to put a real kink on your relationship. People have children for a lot of all the wrong reasons, such as carelessness, lack of planning, beating the biological clock, accidents, pressure from grandparents, evidence of femininity or masculinity, or what have you. When a couple has a child accidentally or otherwise under any of the above circumstances, the child arrives with potentially one strike against him or her. If one member of the couple wants a child and the other doesn't, this is not an ideal emotional atmosphere into which one should bring a life. Granted that the one who wants children might make the ideal parent—if the other parent is not amenable to parenthood or hostile to the idea, chances are that bringing a child into this emotional atmosphere will ultimately do a tremendous disservice to the child. The time to think about the emotional climate (whether parenting is being considered or not) into which a child will be born, is before pregnancy. You, as the adult need to have the best interest of your potential offspring at heart since they do not ask to be born nor do they have any control over the circumstances under which they are born. Two people who genuinely care for each other need first to consider, learn about and understand each other and allow their love to mature and deepen before considering the entrance of a little stranger into the equation. There are no set times or rules for this process. It varies from one individual to another. Understanding that it is in one's favor to experience and grow with a new spouse through at least four to eight season changes, is a good beginning.

CONSISTENCY IN CHILD REARING

Let's assume your relationship is a solid one and you have explored each other's feelings about and agreed upon there being an equal desire to have children. There are a few other considerations that bear further discussion if you are both about raising a happy, healthy and reasonably sane child. It's probable, that if you know your intended really well, you will already be aware of how he or she was raised and the relationship that existed and still exists between him or her and his or her parents. More often than not, the way our parents raised, treated, disciplined, punished or regarded us is unconsciously exercised in the way we deal with our own children. Children, according to their needs, will quickly ascertain the difference between being tolerated or really loved and cared for. Discipline is therefore a particularly sticky subject since too much or too little of it can be germane to the way a child regards him or herself. For instance, if one of you is a very strict disciplinarian or believes in corporal punishment (and one should not confuse discipline with punishment) and the other is more flexible and believes in communication, therein lies a bone of contention that definitely needs to be resolved before considering having children. Agreement on dealing with children's behavior even when the method is not positive, needs to be fairly uniform between parents. A child needs consistency and unity of its parents decisions. It is what gives the child a sense of acceptance and security. In its absence, children quickly learn to become artful dodgers and learn how to play both ends against the middle.

You also need to know, before having children if you (preferably both of you) are going to have and are willing to devote the time needed to accommodate your child or children. Being there is what this all about as far as your kids are concerned. Raising your child or children will take more out of you (and should) for at least 16-18 years of your life than any other endeavor you are likely to undertake. There is no better or more rewarding project than responsibly and lovingly raising another human being.

CHAPTER 12

Compatibility Quiz

Both of you should take this quiz as well as the E.Q. They will give you some insight as to how each of you really feels about different life styles and your attitudes on day to day activities and decisions. Again, there are no "right" answers. But implicit in the questions are degrees of maturity. What is most important is how closely you agree in your responses. The scores that will emerge will only show how each of you feels about each choice.

1) MY FAVORITE TYPE OF MUSIC IS:
    A Cool jazz, Latin ☐
    B Classical, semi classical ☐
    C Country western, folk ☐
    D Rhythm and blues, rock ☐
    E Not interested in music ☐

2) I THINK WE SHOULD HAVE SEX:
    A Every night ☐
    B At least 2 or 3 times a week ☐
    C Once a week ☐
    D A couple of times a month ☐
    E Whenever the mood mutually strikes us ☐

3) ABOUT MY PARTNER'S PLATONIC RELATIONSHIPS:
  A It's okay with me as long as it stays platonic. ☐
  B I think it's a form of temptation and
  should be avoided. ☐
  C I understand it if my partner's interests
  are different from mine. ☐
  D Once I make a commitment, I expect to
  be able to fulfill my partners needs and vice versa.
  That's why I got married. ☐
  E As long as they don't interfere with our relationship
  and it makes my mate happy. ☐

4) MY OPINION OF MARRIAGE IS:
  A You can always get a divorce if it doesn't work out. ☐
  B Once committed, I'm prepared to do
  whatever it takes to stay married. ☐
  C If you really love each other you shouldn't
  have to work at maintaining a marriage. ☐
  D As long as the sex is terrific and exciting
  there's no reason why a marriage shouldn't survive. ☐
  E One has to expect problems and conflicts in
  marriage and if a couple both like and
  love each other they can work them out. ☐

5) ABOUT FINANCES IN A MARRIAGE:
  A One person should handle the money in the
  family preferably the man if he's
  working or making the most money. ☐
  B Each partner should have their own checking
  account, and if working, agree to contribute as
  equally as possible to a joint checking account for
  basic household bills. ☐
  C It's harder when a woman makes more money
  than a man. If she does, she should pay more
  of the bills. ☐

D If only the husband is working,
he should give his wife what he
feels is a fair allowance to run
the house for which she should be
held accountable. ☐

E Each partner should be able to spend
their own money any way they want to
without having to check with their mate. ☐

6) THE BEST WAY TO MAKE LOVE LAST IN A MARRIAGE IS:

A Work at constantly keeping your relationship
romantic, passionate and thrilling. ☐

B Understand that some of the romantic excitement
and passion will gradually fade and are hopefully
replaced with a more mature relaxed, trusting
acceptance of each other. ☐

C Always be totally honest with each other and
discuss even those things that might
hurt with each other. ☐

D Always fight fair while trying to win
your partner over to your point of view. ☐

E Make a marked attempt never to lose your
temper, show anger or raise your voice.
Keep your negative feelings to yourself. ☐

7) MY IDEA OF INTIMACY IS:

A The ability to have a frequent and
dynamic sex life. ☐

B Being vulnerable to each other, sharing
our inner most fantasies or weaknesses
without fear of being ridiculed or criticized. ☐

C Talking with each other and sharing our
feelings about any and everything
that happens to us every day. ☐

D Going everywhere, doing everything
   and spending as much time together
   as possible. ☐
   E Freely sharing all the skeletons in our
   closets and mishaps of the past. ☐

8) WITH REGARDS TO RAISING CHILDREN:
   A A good spanking now and then makes
   right from wrong clear to a child. ☐
   B Children need to be loved and cared
   for unconditionally until 2-3 years of age
   at which point begin discipline by
   communication with them in ways that
   ultimately teaches them self discipline. ☐
   C When children get out of control they
   should be reprimanded soundly then
   deprived of something they want or need
   as punishment. ☐
   D Children shouldn't be disciplined.
   They should be allowed to be free in their
   actions in a well guarded supervised atmosphere
   until they are 5 or 6. ☐
   E Children need to be shown respect for
   their feelings especially when they are
   being disciplined. ☐

9) AS FAR AS CLEANLINESS AND NEATNESS ARE CONCERNED:
   A I am somewhat of a fanatic and am only
   comfortable when things are in their
   proper place and looking their best. ☐
   B I'm pretty casual and tend to let stuff
   pile up before doing a major clean-up. ☐
   C Neatness is not high on my priority list.
   As long as I can find what I'm looking for,
   I'm happy. ☐

    D I'm tidier than most people. I like living in pleasant orderly surroundings. ☐
    E I'm careful about the common areas in the house being neat but my own space is occasionally a mess. ☐

10) I LIKE TO SPEND SUNDAY WITH MY MATE:
    A At home, in and out of bed, eating, reading the Sunday papers and making love. ☐
    B Dressing up and going down town to dinner, and a Broadway play or a movie. ☐
    C Doing some outdoor athletic activity, playing tennis, swimming or going for long walks or a hike in the country. ☐
    D Going to church, sight seeing, to a museum, lecture, symposium, seminar, or other learning activity. ☐
    E Going out to a club for drinks, entertainment and dancing until the wee hours. ☐

Pick the letter that most nearly applies to you. See scoring key in Appendix for your score.

HIS	HERS
1	1
2	2
3	3
4	4
5	5
6	6
7	7
8	8
9	9
10	10
TOTAL_____	**TOTAL**_____

CHAPTER 13

What's Your E.Q.?
(Attitude & Social Consciousness)

Would you like some more clues as to where you might be on the maturity scale?

The following quizzes tap your general feelings as far as your attitude and your social consciousness (both are learned processes) are concerned. There are questions, a blank answer page and keys as to the weight of each question and an evaluation of your ultimate score included.

Keep in mind that your responses and scores on the quiz are not the be all and end all of your personality. Your answers can, however, be clues that will help you understand to some degree how and why you function the way you do assuming you are interested in gaining more information about yourself. There are no "right" answers only ideal answers—which if you picked them all would make you emotionally a very "mature" almost "perfect" person. The object here is for you to learn something about your own true nature. You will have to be very honest about your feelings and then be able to accept the consequences of what this reveals about you. It is the only way you can make a decision to work on yourself or change, should you desire to do so.

Attitude Quiz

1) WHICH DO YOU FEEL IS THE MOST DESIRABLE TRAIT IN A MATURE PERSON:

   A Obedience ☐

   B Intelligence ☐

   C Honesty ☐

   D Compassion ☐

2) WHEN A FRIEND DOES SOMETHING MORE THAN ONCE, OF WHICH YOU THOROUGHLY DISAPPROVE, DO YOU:

   A Dissolve the friendship. ☐

   B Tell them how you feel and limit your contact with them. ☐

   C Act as though it's no concern of yours and carry on as usual. ☐

   D Become very angry with them and show them your contempt in no uncertain terms. ☐

3) WHEN A PERSON OR PERSONS HAVE HURT YOU BADLY OR HAVE DEPRIVED YOU OF SOMETHING MEANINGFUL, YOU REACT IN THE FOLLOWING WAY:

   A You may be able to forgive them later on but you'll never forget it. ☐

   B You would never forgive them or forget it. ☐

   C You would forgive them because its the right thing to do. ☐

   D You would definitely get even and find a way to repay their inconsiderate behavior. ☐

4) IF A GROUP OF CLOSE FRIENDS ARE PLANNING A WEEK-END ACTIVITY AND YOU HAVEN'T BEEN ASKED TO JOIN, WHICH COMES CLOSEST TO YOUR REACTION?

   A You feel hurt and dejected or angry and wonder how they could do this to you. ☐

   B You assume that it was an oversight and

    unless told otherwise assume that you
    are included. ☐
  - **C** You quickly make some other plans so
    you won't appear to be affected and faced with
    an empty week-end. ☐
  - **D** You bring it to their attention and ask for
    an explanation and/or if you can join them. ☐

5) IF IT WERE NECESSARY FOR YOU TO FIND A HOUSE IN A STRANGE NEIGHBORHOOD WHERE THE NUMBERS ARE UNCLEAR, WOULD YOU:

  - **A** Wander up and down the street indefinitely
    looking for someone to approach for help. ☐
  - **B** Ring the first door bell you found and
    ask help from whomever answers. ☐
  - **C** Leave the neighborhood quickly and give
    up trying to find it. ☐
  - **D** Try to find a phone, policemen or an open
    business nearby for help. ☐

6) IF OR WHEN YOU ARE REALLY ANGRY WITH YOUR MATE, FOR WHAT YOU BELIEVE TO BE VALID REASONS, YOU ARE MOST LIKELY TO:

  - **A** Feel somewhat timid about confronting
    your mate or making a scene. ☐
  - **B** Show and/or tell your mate how you feel
    at the first appropriate time and hope
    your mate gets the message. ☐
  - **C** Not feel sure if your anger is warranted
    and test the atmosphere tentatively
    before broaching the subject. ☐
  - **D** Have no fear of lashing out at your mate
    and telling him/her off in no uncertain terms. ☐

7) IF YOUR JOB BEGAN PAYING YOU ONE-QUARTER LESS OF YOUR CURRENT SALARY YOU PROBABLY WOULD:

A Quit immediately and go look for a better paying job. ☐

B Stay on your job and see if you could supplement your income by moonlighting. ☐

C Stay on your job reluctantly even though you hate it because its so hard to find another job. ☐

D Like to stay but financially you have obligations which don't currently allow it. You'd quit but return when things got better. ☐

8) IF A SIBLING OR A CLOSE FRIEND OR MEANINGFUL OTHER REVEALED TO YOU THAT THEY WERE GAY, YOUR REACTION WOULD BE:

A You would feel somewhat deceived or betrayed but would try to understand that there are life styles different from yours. ☐

B To advise the person to get some professional help. ☐

C Probably somewhat surprised but continue to accept him/her and their partner as you would any of your other friends. ☐

D Exercise more caution in your future dealings with the person so they wouldn't get the wrong idea. ☐

9) WHEN YOU'RE IN THE COMPANY OF SOMEONE WHO STRONGLY DISAGREES WITH YOUR VIEWS YOU TEND TO:

A Consider them opinionated and argue with him/her firmly into trying to see it your way. ☐

B Recognize the difficulty in changing another's firmly entrenched beliefs and let it go. ☐

C Enjoy a good argument while trying to

keep your cool and sense of humor. ☐
D Ignore them and what you consider to
be their invalid or incorrect point of view. ☐

10) THERE ARE PEOPLE WHO CALL THEIR PARENTS BY THEIR FIRST NAMES. YOUR FEELINGS ABOUT THIS ARE:

A It's okay if the parents suggest it or ask
their children to do so. ☐
B The idea of children, no matter what their age,
addressing parents by their first names
shows a lack of respect. ☐
C You are not comfortable with the idea. ☐
D If it's comfortable for all parties involved,
why not? ☐

11) IF SOMEONE YOU DON'T KNOW WELL APPEARS TO DISLIKE YOU AND YOU DON'T UNDERSTAND WHY, YOU:

A Realize philosophically that everyone isn't going
to like you and, unless they are threatening,
consider it their problem. ☐
B Consider that chances are they are probably
jealous of you for what you have or who
your are. ☐
C Feel uncomfortable temporarily and,
if no explanation is forthcoming, get past it. ☐
D Wonder what you did to offend them and
how you can change their attitude. ☐

12) ASSUMING YOU CURRENTLY HAVE NO SERIOUS HANDICAPS, HOW DO YOU FEEL ABOUT ALWAYS BEING TAKEN CARE OF?

A God helps those that help themselves.
One should learn to be totally responsible
for oneself and become self-sufficient. ☐

B You need to believe there will always be someone you can count on who will be there to look out for you. ☐

C To some degree yes, but you think you can't trust or expect people to always be there for you. ☐

D To the degree you can look out for yourself, you will. Although you don't expect to be cared for, you wouldn't turn it down if you needed it. ☐

13) IF YOU'RE WAITING ON LINE AND SOMEONE CUTS IN FRONT OF YOU, YOU WOULD MOST LIKELY:

A Not say anything but glare at them furiously for acting as though you don't exist. ☐

B Calmly let them know what they have done, that you don't appreciate it and ask them to move. ☐

C Tell them what kind of person they are and, if necessary, physically retain your space. ☐

D Call attention, if necessary, to their behavior to others on the line since this person has jumped in front of them also. ☐

14) WHICH OF THE FOLLOWING STATEMENTS MOST NEARLY MIRRORS THE WAY YOU FEEL ABOUT YOURSELF?

A Sometimes I feel I could probably do and be better than I am, but I manage to get by okay. ☐

B I could do much better if I were given the chances and opportunities that others have and that I think I deserve. ☐

C I'm aware of my assets and liabilities I try to use my assets well and learn from my liabilities. ☐

D I keep running into bad luck through no fault of my own and that's what slows up my progress. ☐

15) MY ATTITUDE TOWARD BEING AROUND PEOPLE CAN BE SUMMED UP AS FOLLOWS:

A I get along okay with some people but there are others I could really do without. ☐

B I'm at ease with a few well chosen friends. Most types of people are not necessarily worth knowing. ☐

C On the whole I get along with most people who want to get along with me. Otherwise, if I don't enjoy their company I'm indifferent to them. ☐

D Aside from family (and I can do without some of them), I really tend to avoid certain types of people whenever I can. ☐

16) WHICH STATEMENT MOST NEARLY DEFINES HOW YOU FEEL ABOUT YOUR EMPLOYMENT?

A Being gainfully employed is very important. If you don't have a job, people look down on you. ☐

B Since working for most people seems to be the only way to make money honestly, I like to think my job is also satisfying in other ways. ☐

C A job defines who you are. The better the job, the better people will regard and respect you. ☐

D Although it is a way of making money, I'm doing what I like so I don't consider it my job but part of my lifestyle. ☐

17) WHEN SOMEONE OR A SITUATION REALLY ANNOYS YOU FOR NO APPARENT REASON, YOUR GENERAL REACTION IS TO:

A Let those concerned know about it in no uncertain terms and try to put a stop to it. ☐

B Become very hurt and resentful and consider some kind of revenge to repay the affront. ☐

C Be aware of your feelings and then try to find a way of getting away from the aggravation or the event until your feelings moderate. ☐

D Never let the person know they are getting under your skin and tolerate it indefinitely. ☐

18) IF SOMEONE CALLED YOU A DEROGATORY NAME WITH REFERENCE TO YOUR ETHNICITY, GENDER OR LIFESTYLE, YOU WOULD MOST PROBABLY:

A Feel stung and somewhat humiliated by the remark. ☐

B Strike back at them verbally or physically. ☐

C Feel little or no reaction and assume the person has a problem. ☐

D Explain to them how offending the remark is and try to get them to understand how it is injurious to people's feelings. ☐

2) YOUR PLANS FOR A GREATLY ANTICIPATED, LONG PLANNED DATE OR JOINT PROJECT HAVE SUDDENLY BEEN CHANGED OR ENDED BY THE OTHERS INVOLVED. YOUR INITIAL REACTIONS IS:

A One of extreme annoyance at the other person after all the time and energy your have invested. ☐

B Feel somewhat inconvenienced and slowly start wondering what you will do now and how to handle this turn of events. ☐

    C You soon recover from the disappointing news, quickly consider alternative solutions or put another plan into action. ☐
    D Decide never to depend upon another person again because most people are pretty inconsiderate and have no qualms about disappointing you. ☐

3) THE PHILOSOPHY THAT COMES CLOSEST TO YOUR WAY OF THINKING IS:
    A Do unto others before they do unto you. ☐
    B Living well is the best revenge. ☐
    C Don't get mad; get even. ☐
    D The meek shall inherit the face of the earth. ☐

Social Quiz

1) WOMEN'S LIBERATION HAS COME UNDER GREAT SCRUTINY AND CRITICISM AND IS STILL A CONTROVERSIAL SUBJECT. YOUR FEELINGS ABOUT IT ARE:
    A Someone has sold women in general a phony bill of goods. It's still a man's world. ☐
    B The movement appears to have freed the previously unexpressed potential of women. ☐
    C A lot more is expected of women since women's liberation has become a reality. ☐
    D I don't consider it necessarily a positive since it has an emasculating effect on men. ☐

2) WITH REFERENCE TO RELIGION— THE STATEMENT THAT COMES CLOSEST TO YOUR PERSONAL FEELINGS IS:
    A Each individual's feelings for or against religion is personal and really should not be any one else's concern. ☐
    B All children should be taught some kind of religion in order to know about God so as

not offend God. ☐

C The reason this world is in the shape it's in today is because so many people have no religion or do not follow the teachings of God. ☐

D All religious beliefs or the lack of them have something to offer to the person who chooses to follow that particular belief. ☐

3) THE STATEMENT THAT COMES CLOSEST TO YOUR FEELINGS ABOUT GAY RIGHTS IS:

The idea of a gay person teaching my kids in a classroom does not set well with me. ☐

B Although I may not always be comfortable around gays, as long as they don't try to convert me, they should have the same rights as everyone else. ☐

C I'm against gays adopting or having a child whose sexual preference will certainly be influenced by such parents. ☐

D As long as people are ethical and competent, their sexual preference should not deny them rights or access to jobs, public facilities or public office. ☐

4) WHICH STATEMENT ABOUT MARRIAGE MOST NEARLY MIRRORS YOUR OPINION:

A It's really an outdated institution and doesn't serve its original purpose of procreation in which women are involved without marriage. ☐

B Marriage, although it is still the legal lifestyle of couples living together, may not suit the needs of everyone. ☐

C Marriage is sacred and once entered into should be maintained at whatever price, especially where children are involved. ☐

    D Marriage is a commitment and although often difficult and frustrating can have many rewards when really worked at. ☐

5) WHICH OF THE FOUR TOPICS LISTED BELOW WOULD INTEREST YOU AS SUBJECTS OF CONFERENCES BEING HELD:

    A Crime and punishment ☐
    B Repercussions of an unhappy childhood ☐
    C Individual steps of progress toward world peace. ☐
    D Addressing man's inhumanity to man ☐

6) WHICH OF THE FOLLOWING COMES CLOSEST TO HOW YOU FEEL ABOUT THE U.S. SENDING OUR TROOPS INTO COUNTRIES IN CHAOS EVEN THOUGH OUR NATIONAL SECURITY IS NOT THREATENED

    A We cannot say we favor human rights and not intervene when the welfare of the helpless or their civil rights in such countries are being violated. ☐

    B I support a somewhat isolationist policy whereby we let other countries in civil conflict learn how to govern themselves the hard way, if necessary. ☐

    C The U.S. alone, cannot be policeman for the world but we can definitely enlist the aid of other UN forces to help protect the civil rights of all. ☐

    D Its really none of our business when people in other countries squabble with each other. We should steer clear of any such involvement as long as we are not personally threatened. ☐

7) PREVAILING OPINIONS ABOUT ABORTION REMAIN EXTREMELY CONTROVERSIAL AND HAVE BEEN KNOWN TO LEAD TO VIOLENCE, YOUR FEELINGS ABOUT THIS ISSUE ARE:

A It's understandable why the Right to Lifers often have to resort to violent means against offenders to get their point across because all human life is precious. ☐

B The issue is not right to life versus abortion but right to life versus choice for either and that decision should be made only by the person or persons involved. ☐

C It is a grave decision to take a human life. We need laws to protect the unborn by whatever means necessary. ☐

D The choice not to have a child, even if it is considered by others to be a sin, lies in the conscience of the person involved. The government should not interfere. ☐

8) WHEN SOMEONE COMMITS A CAPITAL CRIME SUCH AS RAPE, TREASON OR MURDER, ESPECIALLY THE MURDER OF A PUBLIC OFFICER, YOU BELIEVE THAT PERSON:

A Should definitely receive the death penalty. ☐

B Should spend their life in prison so that every day they're in it will remind them of the gravity of their crime. ☐

C Should be castrated, mutilated or killed in the same way they did their victim. ☐

D Depending on their motivation, criminal record and prospects for rehabilitation, should possibly be punished or imprisoned indefinitely for their act and receive rehabilitative services. ☐

9) WITH REFERENCE TO CHILD REARING, THE STATEMENT THAT COMES CLOSEST TO WHAT YOU BELIEVE IS:

A Children need be taught early on to respect their parents because if you spare the rod, you spoil the child. ☐

B Children need approval and space to express themselves and parents should be pals with them and not show anger or disapproval and allow them a lot of leeway in their behavior. ☐

C The most important things you can give your children are being there for them, unconditional love, non-physical discipline, guidance and control. ☐

D Parenting is often a difficult process and occasional benign punishments and an acute awareness of outside negative influences are necessary to do a good job. ☐

10) WITH REFERENCE TO THE LEGAL SYSTEM MY PERSONAL OPINION IS:

A Some laws that are currently in effect should be broken because they do not serve the best interests of the majority of the people. ☐

B Laws were made to be obeyed and when broken, the perpetrator should be punished regardless. ☐

C If a law is unjust or unfair, by whatever means possible—all efforts should be employed to get rid of it. ☐

D The law is often difficult to apply to everyone and laws should be tempered and mitigated by individual circumstance. ☐

11) YOUR FEELINGS ABOUT PROVIDING HIGHER EDUCATION FOR THE MASSES ARE:

A College is not for everyone. However, our society can and should provide educational institutions and resources in all skills that can tap the potential of all our citizens. ☐

B It's often clear very early on that some students are just not going to make it academically and it would save some time and money by having them enter the work force as early as the law allows. ☐

C Anyone who wants a higher education, whether or not they're college material should be allowed the opportunity. When it becomes too difficult they can always drop out. ☐

D Many successful people (especially in the arts, entertainment, business, etc.) never graduated from high school largely because they pursued the talent or inclination which made them comfortable. ☐

12) EVERYONE HAS AN IDEA OF WHAT THEY MEAN BY SUCCESS. YOUR FEELINGS ABOUT SUCCESS ARE:

A When I have accomplished a planned goal of becoming what I set out to be—ie. doctor, lawyer etc. and am reaping the accompanying rewards for myself and my family, I consider that success. ☐

B When I'm no longer concerned about whether or not I have achieved success and am content with myself and my lifestyle, I consider that success. ☐

C I think success is overrated. Everyone can't be successful or at the top of the heap so it is not that important. ☐

D Being in a position of power and wealth, looked up to, respected and feeling secure in my ability to care for myself and my family is success to me. ☐

13) CONTROVERSY ABOUT THE DEATH PENALTY IN THIS COUNTRY IS STILL VERY PREVALENT. YOUR FEELINGS ABOUT IT ARE:

A If it could be proven that the death penalty was really a deterrent to all other potential murders, I might consider it a viable penalty. ☐

B Of course we should keep the death penalty. It's clearly written in the bible, an eye for an eye, etc. If you can't do the time, don't do the crime. ☐

C Two wrongs don't make a right. Killing another person legally or otherwise for any reason other than of self defense, makes us all less civilized and ethically wrong. ☐

D The death penalty sends a clear message to criminals everywhere as to what their fate will be when they commit this kind of crime. ☐

14) COMPLAINTS ABOUT THE MEDIA (TV, TABLOIDS, MAGAZINES, ETC.) ABOUND ABOUT THE ROLE IT PLAYS IN OUR LIVES AND THE LIVES OF THE FAMOUS. THE OPINION THAT MOST CLOSELY RESEMBLES YOURS IS:

A Once one becomes a celebrity, they should expect intrusive media hype as coming with the territory. They should just learn to take it with a grain of salt. ☐

B The first amendment—Freedom of Speech grants media the right to print, show or write anything they feel they can legally if it's of interest to the public regardless of the consequences. ☐

C The media needs to be muzzled and should not be allowed to reveal a lot of information that is private. There should be laws passed to stop their sensationalizing tactics. ☐

D Everyone, regardless of their prominence in the public eye is entitled to some privacy and at times the media steps over the line which means the burden of maintaining privacy often must rest with the victim. ☐

15) WITH WHICH OF THE STATEMENTS BELOW DO YOU FEEL YOU COULD MOST IDENTIFY:

A It is more important to maintain law and order within society than ensure complete freedom for all. ☐

B Freedom is a responsibility as well as a privilege and it involves knowing its limits especially as it pertains to infringing on the rights of others. ☐

C The concept of freedom is fraudulent in that no one can ever really be free to do whatever they want as there is always someone or something to stop them. ☐

D Freedom is a privilege to be earned and is only for those who know how to use it well and within the confines of the law. ☐

16) MUCH DISCUSSION EVOLVES AROUND OUR WELFARE SYSTEM. YOUR FEELING ABOUT THE CURRENT STATUS OF OUR SOCIAL SERVICES SYSTEM IS:

A If stipends doled out through the public welfare system were decreased or eliminated some of the so called unemployed or unemployable would have to find work. ☐

B Some physical deterrents might be considered in order to discourage or prevent women on welfare from having so many children, who in turn are having children also, thus perpetuating a welfare mentality. ☐

C The welfare system needs a complete overhaul that would include rehabilitative, education and/or

skills training services and should focus
mainly on the needs of children under
the age of sixteen. ☐

D Mothers with dependent children should
take educational and/or skills courses that
can later be put to use in the job market. ☐

17) AMERICANS MANIFEST VARYING DEGREES OF FEELINGS OF PATRIOTISM FOR OUR COUNTRY AND FORM OF GOVERNMENT. WHICH OF THE FOLLOWING COMES CLOSEST TO THE WAY YOU FEEL ABOUT THIS COUNTRY:

A America has the best form of government
on earth. Love it or leave it. ☐

B Our government has its flaws but on the whole,
it seems to work better that other types of
governments around the world. ☐

C Every American citizen's first priority is
their allegiance to our country, America,
our laws and our way of life. ☐

D It's possible to disagree with our country's
policies and still feel patriotism. Though
democracy functions well, the majority is not
always right and the minority is not always wrong. ☐

18) SEX EDUCATION IN THE SCHOOLS HAS BECOME A VERY CONTROVERSIAL ISSUE. THE OPINION THAT COMES CLOSEST TO YOURS IS:

A Most parents are too inept at teaching sex
education at home as well as often being poor
role models so the schools need to start teaching
sex education as early as kindergarten. ☐

B Parents, teachers, PTA of Ed etc. need to resolve
together when and how sex education
should be learned simultaneously at home and
at school since curiosity about sex exists both
inside and outside of the home. ☐

C Sex education should be taught in the privacy of the home by the parents only. It is their right and its up to them as to when and how much their children should know. ☐

D Children's sex education should begin when they start asking questions about sex and answered at their level of understanding. If the parents don't do it, the schools should, especially for youngsters in their early teens. ☐

19) MANY PEOPLE SUFFERING FROM PHOBIAS, PSYCHOSOMATIC ILLNESSES, EMOTIONAL TRAUMAS AND OTHER NEUROSES SEEK AND MANAGE TO FUNCTION WITH THE HELP OF PSYCHOTHERAPY. YOUR THOUGHTS ABOUT THIS PRACTICE ARE:

A People with these kinds of mental afflictions are usually weak willed and simply haven't learned how to control their own lives. ☐

B Therapy is an inexact science and will not help everyone but for those who can make that leap of faith it might be a supportive solution. ☐

C A gifted, ethical, concerned therapist can often succeed in helping a client if the client really acknowledges a need for help and is willing to work toward resolving his\her problems. ☐

D Talking about ones childhood and the past is a waste time gone by and won't solve anything. What these people lack is religion and faith in God. ☐

20) OF THE FOUR IDEAS BELOW FOR THE MAKING OF A BETTER SOCIETY, THE SOLUTION BELOW THAT COMES CLOSEST TO YOUR THINKING IS:

A Sterilization seems justifiable for hardened criminals and or other unfit people who can pass on serious hereditary mental and physical defects and diseases. ☐

B Society is only as good as its weakest link so we need to help all of our underprivileged and downtrodden by way of education and better public services. ☐

C There is no greater resource than our own children and everything should be done to help them grow into healthy mature, tolerant adults, sound in mind and body. ☐

D If we really punished criminals by giving them a dose of their own medicine we'd soon see a reduction in crime and violence which are currently our biggest problems in society. ☐

Circle the letter that most nearly expresses your opinion or feelings. When completed, add up your scores using the scoring sheet in the Appendix. Then refer to the interpretation of scores.

ATTITUDE QUOTIENT

HIS					HERS				
1.	A	B	C	D	1.	A	B	C	D
2.	A	B	C	D	2.	A	B	C	D
3.	A	B	C	D	3.	A	B	C	D
4.	A	B	C	D	4.	A	B	C	D
5.	A	B	C	D	5.	A	B	C	D
6.	A	B	C	D	6.	A	B	C	D
7.	A	B	C	D	7.	A	B	C	D
8.	A	B	C	D	8.	A	B	C	D
9.	A	B	C	D	9.	A	B	C	D
10.	A	B	C	D	10.	A	B	C	D
11.	A	B	C	D	11.	A	B	C	D
12.	A	B	C	D	12.	A	B	C	D
13.	A	B	C	D	13.	A	B	C	D
14.	A	B	C	D	14.	A	B	C	D

15.	A	B	C	D	15.	A	B	C	D
16.	A	B	C	D	16.	A	B	C	D
17.	A	B	C	D	17.	A	B	C	D
18.	A	B	C	D	18.	A	B	C	D
19.	A	B	C	D	19.	A	B	C	D
20.	A	B	C	D	20.	A	B	C	D

Score_____   Score_____

SOCIAL QUOTIENT

HIS   **HERS**

1.	A	B	C	D	1.	A	B	C	D
2.	A	B	C	D	2.	A	B	C	D
3.	A	B	C	D	3.	A	B	C	D
4.	A	B	C	D	4.	A	B	C	D
5.	A	B	C	D	5.	A	B	C	D
6.	A	B	C	D	6.	A	B	C	D
7.	A	B	C	D	7.	A	B	C	D
8.	A	B	C	D	8.	A	B	C	D
9.	A	B	C	D	9.	A	B	C	D
10.	A	B	C	D	10.	A	B	C	D
11.	A	B	C	D	11.	A	B	C	D
12.	A	B	C	D	12.	A	B	C	D
13.	A	B	C	D	13.	A	B	C	D
14.	A	B	C	D	14.	A	B	C	D
15.	A	B	C	D	15.	A	B	C	D
16.	A	B	C	D	16.	A	B	C	D
17.	A	B	C	D	17.	A	B	C	D
18.	A	B	C	D	18.	A	B	C	D
19.	A	B	C	D	19.	A	B	C	D
20.	A	B	C	D	20.	A	B	C	D

Score_____   Score_____

CHAPTER 14

Rules of Thumb for Men Before Considering Marriage

1. YES, MARRIAGE DOES HAVE TO BE WORKED AT, reinvented, improved upon and attended to just as your job or profession does. Your job begins before you make that marital commitment. If you don't agree with this, maybe you should stay alone or at home with mother.

2. BECAUSE MALES ARE MORE ATTRACTED VISUALLY to females—be as sure as possible that you are genuinely comfortable with her looks, size, shape, color etc. Any future destructive (and sometimes even constructive) criticism of you mate's physical attributes will be met with resentment, guilt, embarrassment, deep hurt or just plain misery.

3. LEARN THE IMPORTANCE OF JUST LISTENING, being able to offer a shoulder to cry on and if possible mirroring her feelings rather than jumping into the middle of her complaint with impatience or a solution to what you see as the problem. She will only take such reaction as a need on your part to quickly dispose of a problem you find annoying or a criticism that she is not competent enough to handle the situation herself. Even if and/or when you don't understand what the fuss is all about your attention and focus on her will often gain her undying appreciation.

4. FLEXIBILITY IS A MUST in a good relationship. Don't fear giving into your mate. This is something just between the two of you so no real harm will come of it. It will not make you a wimp to learn how to ignore or at least pay little negative attention to the myriad of imperfections or small errors and indiscretions on her part of which we can all be guilty unless you honestly believe them to be life threatening.

5. NEVER, UNDER ANY CIRCUMSTANCES. STRIKE YOUR MATE (and this goes for both males and females) no matter how unjustly you feel you have been treated, opposed, disrespected, maligned or provoked. Any time you, as a male, feel the need to retaliate physically to a real or imagined indignity from your mate you need to quickly concentrate on and access your feelings rather than act upon them. This is the time for consequential thinking which should help you recognize the position such action will put you in should you follow through on the urge. Chances are you are physically more powerful, bigger and stronger than she is and striking her only proves your brute strength and power over her because you are short on any mental and emotional resources to deal with the provocation. Hitting doesn't make you right, it merely reduces you to a bully who is seriously in need of professional help.

6. LEARN THE TRUE MEANING OF THE WORD "SHARING" especially of yourself and your time. If what she considers important to do or attend to is always secondary to your needs and priorities, it's a message to her that she as well as her interests are not important enough to compete with you and yours respectively. It's still necessary that each of you give the other space to pursue individual interests but in marriage it's greatly appreciated by your mate if you find some activities and interest of hers with which you are comfortable and can enjoy as much as she does.

7. WOMEN ARE GENERALLY ROMANCE PRONE aside from all the other vast differences physical, biological, psychological and emotional between men and women. However competent or business like women can be or are portrayed they still harbor romantic illusions of what a relationship and their mate should be like. This illusion is so often perpetuated by men themselves by way of romantic love songs, sensuously sung by men which fuel women's emotions with overwhelming expectations of what loving and being in love is all about. Females have a great deal of difficulty understanding how romantic males can be in the movies, books, plays, on TV and before marriage and how, after which, they often do a 180 degree turn around.

One of my female clients made the complaint that when she confronted her husband of two years with the question "How come you were so gallant, thoughtful and attentive to me before we got married. There was nothing you wouldn't do to please me then." She stated her husband calmly replied "Well, I was trying to get you then." There's a message in that reply to which my client should have listened. She's presumably the same person he married—is she no longer worthy of his attention—and was she ever except as a means to an end? The smallest romantic overtures done on a consistent or regular basis won't necessarily make for a torrid or whirlwind affair but they will certainly keep the bitterness, disappointment and feelings of rejection at bay. A solicitous or sexy call in the middle of the day, a small gift, poem, single rose, a book, a foot massage, suggestions for spending the night at a hotel in town can set the stage for lots of very promising evenings. Try bringing home a fully cooked dinner candles and all, a walk in the park hand in hand sharing the days or weeks activities, a getaway weekend to the country or out of the country if you can afford it. Actually most women need very little incentive to be favorably disposed to their mates. It really is the thought that counts.

8. START THINKING BEFORE MARRIAGE about the role women are playing in the world today. Because so many women are out in the work force today (and even if they're not, they may be a mother or a household engineer, more often both) their work truly is never done. Nothing makes a woman feel more appreciated than when her mate volunteers (not has to be subtly prodded, tricked, nagged or dragged kicking and screaming) to help with or share household chores. If you feel there are some duties or work not compatible with your male image then opt for other chores you can do to alleviate her burden rather than either complain about the state the house is in or worse, do nothing.

It's call lighting a candle rather than cursing the darkness. This kind of consideration is often a prelude to future romantic encounters and can definitely spice up your sex life. If you want something from someone, find out what it is they want or need and give it to them first. It's all about enlightened self-interest again.

9. ONE OF THE MOST FREQUENT COMPLAINTS many of my female clients have about men they see as partners in a potential relationship is their lack of common courtesy and consideration. A good example is a female client, about 42 years of age, very attractive was dating a gentlemen for about six months. She is emotionally mature and had maintained a slow paced relationship until she felt, thru his behavior and declarations, that he was genuinely interested in her and cared deeply for her. After six months, they did have sexual relations which they mutually experienced as more than satisfactory and when she last saw him they parted on what appeared to be on the best of terms. This included a mutual understanding that they would see each other very soon thereafter. Over a week went by and she did not hear from him, leading her to at least briefly have all sorts of self doubt, self recriminations and feelings of stupidity about her unmet expectations. She went through some mildly agonizing trips of believing it was something she had done or that this was somehow her fault while being helped to understand the nature of men being that often they do not attach the same significance or importance to a sexual encounter as women do, even when it's with someone for whom they have strong feelings. In some cases the encounter has helped them feel either closer, obligated or more committed to the female of their choice and it frightens them to have such strong feelings in that it may rob them of their autonomy. In other instances they may simply forget or put aside contacting their partner over a protracted period of time because their work or other projects have taken precedence in their lives. Last but not necessarily least, they may decide they do not want to continue the relationship for reasons that my have nothing to do with their lover.

As it turned out, my female client quickly recuperated and made a conscious decision to enjoy the whole episode for what it was worth realizing she had always been consciously aware of whatever consequences might occur. As it turned out, her partner did contact her two weeks later. She didn't feel she could mention any of this to him but acknowledged that she maintained a cautious distance with him for quite some time before she felt comfortable with him again.

Regardless of the reason, not to call or contact in some way someone with whom you have shared a sexual encounter (assuming it was not a mutually agreed upon one night stand or an encounter with a prostitute) within a matter of days, is tacky, discourteous or downright cowardly—depending on your reason. If your partner is someone you really care about you should learn how to mirror her feelings about how she experiences this kind of behavior. You will not endear yourself to her if you don't make contact within a reasonable period of time or expect a possibly chilly reception when you do, which should not come as a surprise. This behavior lacks class before you marry so even if you don't wish to pursue the relationship—it's a sign of maturity to still call or in some way reach your partner with your misgivings or whatever feelings you may have within days after having shared sexually intimate relations with her.

CHAPTER 15

Rules of Thumb for Females Before Considering Marriage

1. WHAT MAKES YOUR MAN TICK? The sooner you find the answer to this question the easier it will be for you to provide it, if you wish. There are a few things you will find that make most men tick not the least of which is his need to feel important and well appreciated, especially by you. There are at least three stand out areas for your man which if he doesn't feel in command will result in a poor atmosphere in which he can function ably as a part of a couple: his prowess in his sex life, his occupation or profession and his financial life, not necessarily in that order. He needs to feel not only confident but comfortable within himself and also that you perceive him as being very acceptable or special in at least these three areas.

2. KNOW SOMETHING ABOUT WHAT YOU CURRENTLY WANT in a man before narrowing down your choices to one. Deciding to make a permanent commitment because your intended has the "potential" to ultimately become what you want him to be or to live up to your expectations is a very risky business: Sometimes this turns out to be many disappointing years of frustration as he tries unsuccessfully to actualize that potential especially if or while depending upon your resources. He may not help feeling that he does not or cannot contribute his fair share of what you feel is needed to maintain a relationship between you. It is much more difficult to appreciate what a person can do rather than what they are actually doing or have already done.

3. LEARN HOW TO DEAL WITH YOUR NEGATIVE FEELINGS especially where your mate is concerned. This does not mean you need to deny anger, annoyance, irritability or even feelings of fury. It means you need to understand that these are your feelings and you are really the only one who can resolve them. So before dumping them on your mate even if he has provoked them, or anyone else, recognize that it's hard to be rational when you're very angry so you need to wait until these feelings subside—using whatever tactics you can to maintain a calm or silent visage. Go for a walk or, get away from the scene physically, if possible. If your mate wants to know what's wrong, as calmly as possible let him know you need to think thru your feelings before you share them with him.

Men can be reached better indirectly and calmly than through the onslaught inherent in direct confrontation.

4. WHENEVER LODGING A COMPLAINT especially against your mate, even when you believe you have actual facts at your disposal, the message you want to get across is how what you are complaining about has made you feel. Facts can be disputed, argued about or denied, feelings can't. What's done is done but how you feel about it goes on until what you feel is somehow acknowledged or recognized or at least some contribution toward resolution has been offered by your partner. If your mate commits the same harmful boo boo again and again before you decide to marry (already knowing the negative repercussions as to how this has made you feel) there's a clear message there. His need to repeat what he's doing is more important to him than how you feel about it. You can take it from there as to whether or not you can sustain this kind of in-your-face treatment. After marriage, chances are the behavior won't change. The key here is not to become a basket case because of his behavior. As an adult, he has a right to be a heel or a louse or pursue the negative behavior if he wants to. You, on the other hand also have the right not to tolerate the resulting hurt feelings it creates. You will need to find as gentle a way as possible to communicate this to your mate.

5. THINK IN TERMS OF ACCENTUATING THE POSITIVE and eliminating or at least paying less attention to the negative. One of the ways of dealing successfully with children is to understand how badly they need attention and they don't care whether its positive or negative as long as they are not being ignored. It behooves a thinking parent to acknowledge and praise any positive behavior or accomplishment in which their child is involved and unless it is something terribly dangerous, to ignore or down play their negative behavior as often as possible. There is a child in all of us that each of us will marry as well as the adult you see on a daily basis.

6. BY NOW YOU HAVE AT LEAST A VAGUE IDEA that men are generally decision and action prone, don't like to be victimized by one-upmanship, don't deal well with criticism and/or direct angry confrontation—especially from women. So how do you approach your partner with something that is seriously problematic to you? How do you get him to understand your needs, your point of view or your feelings without alienating him, turning him off or having him tune you out? A good start is understanding timing. Thinking in terms of the time you will need to take for preparation of your complaint and the best time you can find to present it to him are two factors that can help you to be successful. Give yourself time to diffuse your own feelings so you can think about, prepare and present the problem calmly and rationally. Pick a time when his mood is good or up and he is reasonably rested and comfortable. Be prepared for opposition, misunderstanding, artful dodging or denial all of which will need to be handled calmly as you stick to your guns. Assuming he is not a Neanderthal, you should be able to get your point successfully across or at least listened to. You may need to go thru several of these scenarios to experience the pattern of his reactions. In any case, you have set the stage for such future discussions that are bound to arise, before you have decided to marry.

7. MEN ARE INTO QUANTITY and women are into quality. Keep in mind that men can reproduce a hundred times more sperm than women who produce only a single egg each month. So men will generally have intercourse with whoever or in some cases whatever is warm and willing coming down the pike without regard as to what she may or may not produce. Females, therefore generally don't give birth more than once a year—depending on when they get pregnant—so they are more concerned about the quality of a potential mate, and well they should be before getting involved in what can potentially put them thru a nine month ordeal of creating another human being. If you are concerned about getting married and having children, long before you get to that point in your marriage where you begin to blame the negative traits of your children on what you believe they have inherited from their father's gene pool, you need to be very selective about your choice of a mate.

8. AN EYE FOR AN EYE, and a tooth for a tooth only leaves a lot of people disabled. When we seek revenge or to give back in kind what has happened to us—there are no holds barred for the recipient of your revenge as far as their striking back at us again. Using sex as a weapon, by way of withdrawal as punishment, a revenge tactic or to assuage hurt feelings is the beginning of undermining any relationship. It can open up a Pandora's box of retaliation that you might rather not deal with. It can hardly be translated by him in any other way than that you are rejecting him totally. The trick here is to isolate the offensive deed from the person himself and address what he has done not who or what he is. He will need to know how this has affected you to the extent that you feel the way you do. Nobody expects that you will always be ready, willing and able for sexual intimacy or that you will always be completely pleased with your potential spouse. You will in all probability have flare-ups that will leave you smoldering to the point that you don't want your mate anywhere near you. However, again you will need time to separate the deed from him so you can address the deed more clearly. It will be your choice to also explain why at that moment (should the occasion arise) that you would be uncomfortable sharing sexual intimacy without closing the door on the idea. The object here is to give you a chance to attempt to resolve the situation so your feelings of avoidance are only temporary and with the proper recognition and handling will diminish. One of the more feminine loveable traits is the art of being graceful and no matter what the outcome of your dilemma is, you will always feel much better about yourself if you have handled yourself well. Getting into the habit of "grace under fire" and practicing your ability to carry it off before you decide to marry will go a long way toward dealing with any number of sticky situations after marriage.

A RULE OF THUMB FOR BOTH SEXES
Clearly what appears to be important between couples are not only the similarities they share, but even more so the ability to compromise, accept, tolerate or go along, without resentment with the small and sometimes larger annoyances which are results of the differences that are bound to exist between two different sexes who are working at living with each other. All these small hourly and daily considerations of each other are forms of making love to each other all day long so that by the time evening rolls around, hopefully the pump has been primed for romantic spontaneity.

CHAPTER 16

Off The Cuff (The way I see it)

If nothing else, by now the reader has gotten the idea of how different socially, biologically emotionally and physiologically the sexes are. Yet both genders have one thing in common—even though they may express it differently. Everyone needs to feel at some time or other that they are really loved. Offshoots of this desire are the need to feel wanted, needed, respected, admired or at least acknowledged—any or all of which are (or have to be substitutes for) the real thing. Love, for so many seems so elusive especially for adults. Most of us get at least a small portion of genuine caring or one or more of the substitutes at different times in our lives and realize we have to make do until we luck up on that real thing. After babyhood and childhood when most all of us were loveable, with little or no effort on our part, we needed to learn how to either make or keep ourselves loveable as we grew into adulthood. Granted, everyone is not going to love us, but how do the two sexes deal with not only making and keeping themselves loveable to each other but also receive from their partners behavior that also makes them feel important and loved?

SEXUAL DYSFUNCTION

A recent survey shows that 31% of men suffer from some type of sexual dysfunction i.e., loss of ability, desire, inclination and or interest. Among women the figure is higher at 43%. The most prominent reasons for the malaise among men appears to be stress from over work, too busy a schedule, inability to extract themselves from the rat race, physical deterioration due to excessive use of drugs, alcohol, tobacco or some type of unresolved trauma or mental conditioning during their earlier years. The reason for the higher percentage of sexual impairment among women which includes some or all of the above is reportedly due to the lack of a quality relationship with men in general and often their mates in particular. It appears that to some degree the former reasons feed into the latter ones.

TRUE FRIENDSHIP NEEDS TO BE ADDED TO THE MIX
Let's for a moment look at it from the male point of view. Warm, giving, surrendering and totally abandoned sex from his female partner is generally what makes a man feel competent, important loved and wanted even if he's not capable of, nor inclined to return the feeling, après ski. This, in large part, appears to be due to the fact that most men do not necessarily confuse sex with love and are quite capable of performing mind-boggling sex with their female partners without the added burden of having to feel love for them. Unfortunately, many or most women, especially those who are supersensitive, are of a giving nature, and are still very much in touch with themselves will go through periods of lacking sexual desire because they do equate sex with love. No matter how mature they are they need to feel they are unconditionally acceptable and loved in order to become vulnerable, perform and utterly surrender themselves to sexual abandon with their mates. The message here seems to be that even if you do not fall into either or any of these categories, each partner needs to learn what it takes to make their mate feel loved and loveable. And what is the catalyst that brings this about? We're back to that old saw "communication," verbal or otherwise with one difference. True friendship needs to be added to the mix and all that it implies implicitly and explicitly. While you are still in the single state, the most important quality you will need to develop is a genuine liking, acceptance of, and tolerance for your potential spouse. This may or may not develop into a grand passion, a no holds barred love affair or permanent commitment.

REAL FRIENDS

Real friends of either the same or opposite sex watch each other's back, are generous with each other, are loyal, dependable, trustworthy and are there for each other, no matter what. A real friend behaves toward you in a fashion that makes you feel loved wanted and important to them and real friends have no difficulty in letting each other know how they feel. They can gauge your emotional mood, know when to intrude or retreat, usually listen well to you, tolerate your idiosyncrasies (often finding them more amusing than irritating) and like and enjoy spending time with you sharing the things you both like to do. A true friend is someone whom you can criticize (preferably constructively) and be criticized by as well as to whom you can give and from whom you can also receive advice without feeling superior, threatened, diminished or rejected, respectively.

RIGHT BRAIN LEFT BRAIN

It appears these traits and the ability to maintain friendships is more prevalent among women than men. Research studies at the University of Vermont College of Medicine suggest that women have more neurons in the temporal lobe which relates to learning, complete memory, emotional response and intuition, than men. Men are often baffled by how empathetically women can relate to each other even when they disagree or are at odds with each other. Because of their competitive nature and having a differently constructed corpus callasum which crosses messages between the right and the left hemispheres of their brains men are somewhat the losers in their ability to use both sides of their brains simultaneously. This appears to be a feat of which women are physiologically capable in that they are tuned into their right brain intuitive signals while they are performing left brain rational tasks. Ironically that leaves a woman the task of having to be more willing to explore and work at a relationship simply because she is better socially, psychologically and physiologically equipped to do so. Doesn't seem fair, does it?

IS MARRIAGE WORTH THE EFFORT?

That brings us, particularly women, to the question of what does one do about this inequality in the amount of effort needed to be put forth to build and sustain a relationship. It appears to boil down to first deciding (as you would do before beginning any project you feel is going to be worth the effort) if you really want a relationship with this person considering what you may perceive as all of his emotional deficits. There was a time when women generally didn't have the option of openly asking this question and those that did were viewed with suspicion or disdain. Getting a man to marry you at any or all costs was the trend of the day and for some women still is. But now women have evolved to a point where they can ask themselves, is getting a man worth what it's going to cost. They need to already know if they are really prepared to put forth the time, energy patience and effort it will take to attract, please and understand a potential partner and that's only the beginning. They need to also consider partially giving up their privacy while continuously building closeness in an effort to sustain and cement a relationship. However you might answer this, you clearly have a choice and it's yours to make.

NON-MARRIAGE IS AN OPTION

Rather than complain about men being the way they are and about your having to do most of the work and understanding that will be required in a thriving relationship you can recognize that you are capable of having a fulfilling life without a man or a husband. This is an especially rewarding realization if it is preferable to risking heartache or you have previously experienced a negative or an emotionally devastating relationship. It's always a trade-off.

Next question: If this is unthinkable, assume you are willing to take on this responsibility (which is largely a responsibility to yourself). You realize all the goodies you have stored up to spend on some unsuspecting male, what do you do now? Shouldn't your choice be someone who already has most of the qualities you are seeking and worth what you think you have to offer? If all men are clods, why not on a scale of one to ten choose an eight, nine or ten clod versus a two clod. However one sided this all has begun to sound, its not meant to be this way. Of course, all men are not alike and there are guys out there who really do have a lot of sensitivity, the ability to care and share, are willing to work at a relationship and are not commitment phobic. They do exist, not in large percentages, but they do exist. And on the same side of the coin there are women out there who are commitment phobic, insensitive, selfish, difficult to understand or work with and down right bitchy. The predictions and options work both ways. So the same, of course, is true for men choosing their mates except that their criteria for women is usually more visual and at the onset, more superficial. They are therefore often not really emotionally prepared for when the wrapping comes off. Men therefore also need to look deeper into their own emotional make-ups and needs—even if they are not generally prone to do so.

WOMEN READERS

More women than men will probably be interested in the context of this book—by the very nature of what has been explained in previous chapters. In most cases, if men do get around to reading or even being vaguely interested, it will be at the behest or urging of a female. True, the information contained herein is slanted towards and more focused on women. A smart man who is really serious about bonding with his mate and maintaining a great relationship with her will hopefully absorb some of this information as a form of enlightened self-interest. But since women are probably going to have to put forth the most effort to be the more understanding of the two it only seems fair that she should also have more support in doing so. If this is true, then there are some cautions and precautions which, when considered, will hopefully help her in her task.

She, more than her counterpart (no matter how fragile his ego is) needs to know who and what she is and was (without flaunting or denying it) before getting into a relationship. Should the affair prove to be disastrous, she will have her good, reasonably complete self to return to. That self will help her pick up the pieces, learn from her mistakes, reflect and still maintain the capacity to start all over again. This is eminently better than diving into a pool of self-destructive behavior. She needs to have high self-esteem not acquired through her identity with him or any other male and be able to recognize and appreciate her own self worth. She must also know how to hold onto her unasked for or unsolicited emotions, and expressions of generosity. At the same time, she needs to realize that there is a part of her (her pilot light if you will) that will never be shared with anyone except herself. This is a recognition that women should have of themselves long before they enter any relationship. Many women in their eagerness to please, or to make many others comfortable, do so in order to assure themselves they are making their presence more predominantly felt. The key to remaining on good terms with yourself is pacing yourself by generally keeping your distance until invited to come closer or until your counterpart is on your turf.

EMOTIONAL HEALTH

This is not game playing. It's the preservation of your emotional health and self. As the comics say, always leave them laughing and or asking for or wanting more which is barely possible to offer if there's nothing left to give. If you, as a female, have a good handle on yourself and are independent enough to provide for most of your own needs you will not be tempted or drawn in by charm, baubles, promises, riches or threats. You will be more than willing to wait for a person of emotional substance who will complement and enhance what you already are and have. You will also recognize how important it is for your choice of a mate to have a really solid, reputable character. It takes time and observation beyond the surface to ascertain a person's character as to his trustworthiness, dependability, fidelity and sincerity. Keep in mind men's sexual prowess, their earning ability and the amount of power and control they can exercise over their environment are hallmarks of their personality. When they are willing to share these things with you by way of gifts or demonstration, that does not mean they can't also have good character but—it definitely doesn't mean that they have either. Sometimes sharing largesse with you is a cover up for lack of character or generosity of spirit so women should probably think twice before being lured into a relationship based on such superficial offerings. It's a given that men proffer material things as proof of their affection and or ability to provide for and support. Since this is generally true anyway, the trick is to tune into your own intuition and inner needs to find someone who is also emotionally mature and is of sterling character even if he does not have great wealth or position. He will ultimately be more appreciated, acceptable and cherished by you in the long run. Men reading this might get a clue that they may need to cultivate more than their good looks, financial status or sexual expertise if they want a woman of quality. These musings work both ways, incidentally, depending upon which partner needs additional character building. Unfortunately once one perceives oneself as an adult it's difficult for them to recognize that their behavior, character and attitude need upgrading, much less being able to change or improve it. Therefore it behooves members of both sexes to take their time in ascertaining, not only what they're looking for in another but also what they're offering to their prospective mates. Happy Hunting!

APPENDIX

The object of this quiz is to see how closely your scores coincide and how similar your total scores are.

COMPATIBILITY SCORING KEY

1.	A (5)	B (4)	C (3)	D (2)	E (1)
2.	A (4)	B (2)	C (3)	D (1)	E (5)
3.	A (3)	B (1)	C (4)	D (2)	E (5)
4	A (1)	B (4)	C (2)	D (3)	E (5)
5	A (1)	B (5)	C (2)	D (3)	E (4)
6	A (2)	B (5)	C (3)	D (4)	E (1)
7.	A (1)	B (5)	C (4)	D (3)	E (2)
8.	A (1)	B (5)	C (2)	D (3)	E (4)
9.	A (1)	B (3)	C (2)	D (5)	E (4)
10.	A (5)	B (2)	C (4)	D (3)	E (1)

A.Q. SCORING KEY

1.	A (0)	B (2)	C (5)	D (10)
2.	A (2)	B (10)	C (5)	D (0)
3.	A (10)	B (5)	C (5)	D (2)
4.	A (0)	B (5)	C (2)	D (10)
5.	A (0)	B (2)	C (5)	D (10)
6.	A (0)	B (10)	C (5)	D (2)
7.	A (2)	B (5)	C (0)	D (10)
8.	A (5)	B (0)	C (10)	D (2)

9.	A (2)	B (10)	C (5)	D (0)
10.	A (5)	B (0)	C (2)	D (10)
11.	A (10)	B (2)	C (5)	D (0)
12.	A (5)	B (0)	C (2)	D (10)
13.	A (2)	B (10)	C (0)	D (5)
14.	A (5)	B (0)	C (10)	D (2)
15.	A (5)	B (2)	C (10)	D (0)
16.	A (2)	B (5)	C (0)	D (10)
17.	A (5)	B (2)	C (10)	D (2)
18.	A (0)	B (2)	C (10)	D (5)
19.	A (2)	B (5)	C (10)	D (0)
20.	A (2)	B (10)	C (5)	D (0)

A.Q.—INTERPRETATION OF SCORES FOR FACILITATORS

150–200 If you have scored an A.Q. in this range you appear to be very mature and seemingly willing to accept responsibility for the shape your life has taken. You are self-motivated and your feelings of self-worth and selfesteem appear to be high. You seem to be able to maintain a consistency and balance in your sense of values and in your capacity to tolerate, give and receive.

125-149 Most people will fall into this range of A.Q. which represents a striving for and movement toward maturity. You generally stay within safe limits of tolerance and self-acceptance but still have a few emotions that may act as obstacles to your ongoing progress and in your relationships. Nevertheless, you appear to always be seeking higher emotional ground and to "do the right thing."

100-124 If your A.Q. is in this range, your have a tendency to seek or attract negative excitement, and to create stress for yourself because of unmet needs or demands made on those external to yourself. You may feel overwhelmed by expectations of others as well as quite resentful of the "powers that be," maybe justifiably. If you recognize this, that's half the trip toward becoming a more mature adult.

0–99 If you have indeed scored this low, your self-esteem and feelings of personal responsibility for your attitude both need some inner investigating. You appear to be quite emotionally immature and somewhat vindictive, possibly because of negative upbringing. You might want to talk with someone you trust and to whom you could ventilate your feelings and where you could also get some productive feedback.

S.Q. SCORING KEY

1. A (2)   B (10) C (5)   D (0)
2. A (10) B (2)   C (0)   D (5)
3. B (10) D (5)   C (2)   A (0)
4. A (0)   B (5)   C (2)   D (10)
5. A (0)   B (2)   C (10) D (5)
6. A (5)   B (2)   C (10) D (0)
7. A (2)   B (10) C (0)   D (5)
8. A (0)   B (5)   C (2)   D (10)
9. A (0)   B (2)   C (10) D (5)
10. A (2)   B (0)   C (5)   D (10)
11. A (10) B (0)   C (2)   D (5)
12. A (5)   B (10) C (2)   D (0)
13. A (5)   B (0)   C (10) D (2)
14. A (5)   B (0)   C (2)   D (10)
15. A (2)   B (10) C (0)   D (5)
16. A (2)   B (0)   C (10) D (5)
17. A (0)   B (5)   C (2)   D (10)
18. A (2)   B (10) C (0)   D (5)
19. A (2)   B (5)   C (10) D (0)
20. A (0)   B (5)   C (10) D (2)

S.Q.—INTERPRETATION OF SCORES FOR FACILITATORS

150–200 This range of S.Q. represents a liberal, compassionate, and flexible sense of social values. You appear to be fair and objective on social issues, empathetically always considering both sides while still maintaining your own beliefs and self-interest. You can allow for others' attitudes and differences and still be comfortable with yourself. You indicate by your responses that you tend to deal ethically, morally and humanely with the real world.

125–149 Although you may have been conditioned to have certain attitudes about social issues, you are still attempting to be humane when it comes to judging or acting upon social issues. Most people fall into this average range of the ethically motivated who still need to feel safe when they cease following negative rules or attitudes gathered from their parents or others who have taught them. You might want to review those questions that mirror your feelings on understanding and having compassion for your fellow human beings.

100 –124 Your S.Q. falls into the low average range of sensitivity and fairness to your fellow human beings. You appear to be somewhat rigid and authoritarian in your outlook and may find it difficult to identify with human frailty or those less fortunate that yourself. You might want to do some inner scanning and find out why you have so little space to deal with understanding, changes and transitions, gracefully.

0–99 If you have really scored in this low range, you appear to have a definite deficit in our ability to identify with others. You responses are those of a malcontent who is quite reactionary and punitive and is more concerned with being an authority, and with retribution than with seeking applicable solutions.

www.ingramcontent.com/pod-product-compliance
Lightning Source LLC
LaVergne TN
LVHW040151080526
838202LV00042B/3113